Pig

Animal
Series editor: Jonathan Burt

Already published

Crow
Boria Sax

Tiger
Susie Green

Elephant
Dan Wylie

Ant
Charlotte Sleigh

Salmon
Peter Coates

Eel
Richard Schweid

Tortoise
Peter Young

Fox
Martin Wallen

Ape
John Sorenson

Cockroach
Marion Copeland

Fly
Steven Connor

Penguin
Stephen Martin

Dog
Susan McHugh

Cat
Katharine M. Rogers

Owl
Desmond Morris

Oyster
Rebecca Stott

Peacock
Christine E. Jackson

Pigeon
Barbara Allen

Bear
Robert E. Bieder

Cow
Hannah Velten

Snail
Peter Williams

Bee
Claire Preston

Swan
Peter Young

Hare
Simon Carnell

Rat
Jonathan Burt

Shark
Dean Crawford

Lion
Deirdre Jackson

Snake
Drake Stutesman

Duck
Victoria de Rijke

Camel
Robert Irwin

Falcon
Helen Macdonald

Rhinoceros
Kelly Enright

Giraffe
Edgar Williams

Whale
Joe Roman

Horse
Elaine Walker

Lobster
Richard J. King

Parrot
Paul Carter

Moose
Kevin Jackson

Pig

Brett Mizelle

REAKTION BOOKS

For my mother, Marion Jones Nairn Mizelle

Published by
REAKTION BOOKS LTD
33 Great Sutton Street
London EC1V 0DX, UK
www.reaktionbooks.co.uk

First published 2011
Copyright © Brett Mizelle 2011

Printed and bound in China

British Library Cataloguing in Publication Data
Mizelle, Brett.
Pig. – (Animal)
1. Suidae. 2. Swine. 3. Swine as laboratory animals.
4. Pork industry and trade. 5. Swine in literature.
6. Swine in art.
I. Title II. Series
599.6'33-DC22

ISBN: 978 1 86189 805 0

Contents

Preface

Pigs are ubiquitous in the modern world, whether we are talking about the more than one billion domesticated pigs on the planet or the countless representations of pigs and 'piggishness' that circulate through most of the world's cultures. The pig is an animal that seems well enough known: who, after all, does not know what a pig is or knows what it means to call someone a 'pig'?

As it turns out, however, pigs – as both living animals and as symbols – deserve a second look, a reconsideration of both their unique talents and their contribution to human history. While a comprehensive history of the extensive, varied and complicated human–pig relationship is impossible, I hope to show that pigs are more than just the 18 per cent ham, 16 per cent bacon, 15 per cent loin, 12 per cent fatback, 10 per cent lard and 3 per cent each of spare rib, plate, jowl, foot and trimmings that exit the modern packing plant. After all, pigs have been structurally and symbolically significant in the making of human society and culture across the globe. Pigs have fed us, entertained us and provided us with ways to think about our relationships with each other on this porcine planet.

The pig has also been shaped by its long relationship with humans. Evolution and human intervention have led to the development of more than 500 breeds and varieties of pigs that

can be found on every continent except Antarctica. In addition to their use as food, pigs have been subjects of medical experimentation and bred to provide 'spare parts' for humans, as there are numerous similarities between human and pig physiology. In an interesting paradox, however, the more pigs there are in the world, the harder it has become to see them. Although living pigs used to be familiar in a number of social environments, over time, especially in developed nations, they have vanished from view. Recent developments in the way pork is produced

Daughter of resettlement client, San Luis Valley Farms, Alamosa, Colorado, poses with two of her father's fine pigs', c. 1939. The US government relocated about 10,000 impoverished farming families to more promising land during the New Deal.

8

'Farmer John' mural, Clougherty Meat Packing Co., Vernon, California, 1960s.

have severed many of the historical connections between humans and pigs, and along with the multiple ways in which we consume the 'cultural' pig or the 'idea of the pig', have obscured the actual animal.

This occlusion of the real experiences of pigs, animals which we consume as pork and think about and with as representations and symbols, can be seen in an industrial neighbourhood in Los Angeles, where happy and healthy pigs frolic in an idyllic setting. Some are lazing on the grass in the sun. Others are drinking from a stream or eating at a trough. A buxom country girl, bursting out of her clothes, leads one on a rope. Another pig is decked out in sunglasses and baseball cap, piloting a small plane towing a banner featuring the logo of the Farmer John Brand, 'family owned since 1931'. These pigs are the stars of the murals that decorate the walls of the Clougherty Meat Packing Company plant in Vernon, California.[1] The contradiction between the murals, with their nostalgic representations of

Sue Coe, *Los Angeles Farmer Johns Packing plant, 6 pm. Worker Waits for Bus, Oct. '88*, 1995, mixed media on paper.

pigs in the countryside, and the killing of pigs that takes place inside this labour-intensive factory in the industrial urban landscape, should come as no surprise. In fact the activist artist Sue Coe has brought this tension to the surface in several of her paintings and drawings, which focus on the intertwined suffering of humans and animals at Farmer John's.[2] Yet these paintings of contented pigs have both appeal and power, for they mark our complicated and ambivalent human attitudes about and practices towards pigs. They remind us of a human–pig relationship that despite being almost always centred on the killing of the latter by the former, was not always so distanced or as alienated as it is in the industrialized world today. Perhaps more than ever, then, we need to retrieve the pig from both its end products and its symbolic and representational ubiquity and rethink, or even reform, that relationship.

1 What is a Pig?

One would think that the problem of defining the pig would be a minor one. In fact, because of the global ubiquity of pigs, most humans have some idea about what a pig is. Millions of people have 'drawn a pig' as part of an online personality test. As you might guess, these pigs have a thick body, short legs, a snout for a nose, small eyes and a small corkscrew-shaped tail. Although the drawings on this website are black and white, I would bet that most imagine their pig – always a domestic rather than a wild or feral animal – as being pinkish in colour.[1]

Scientists, on the other hand, have a much more specific definition of the pig. In descending order, pigs belong to the kingdom *animalia*, phylum *chordata*, order *artiodactyla* (even-toed ungulates) and family *suidae*. There are sixteen living species of wild hogs and pigs within the family *suidae*, divided further by region. For example, there are five kinds of African pigs (including the Bush Pig, Red River Hog, Forest Hog and two species of Warthog), three American pigs (or Peccaries), and six species of pigs found in the Pacific Islands. There are two species of Eurasian pigs, the endangered Pygmy Hog (now largely confined to a few individuals in the Indian state of Assam) and, most significant for our purposes, the Wild Boar (*Sus scrofa*), the ancestor of all breeds of domestic pigs (*S. s. domesticus*).

A domestic pig (*Sus scrofa domesticus*) on an organic farm in Switzerland.

Today's pigs are distant descendants of the proto-pigs, or Entelodonts, that date back almost 40 million years and first appeared in Asia before migrating to Europe and the Americas. These Entelodonts were, like modern pigs, omnivorous, with short slender legs, bulky bodies and a long muzzle. The two largest of these proto-pigs, North America's *Daeodon shoshoensis* and the Eurasian *Paraentelodon intermedium*, stood up to 215 cm (7 feet) tall and were powerful predators for approximately 20 million years.[2]

Their successors became smaller and faster as they adapted to changing times and environments. The wild boar in particular was an important prey animal for hunter-gatherers across Eurasia for millennia. This predator–prey relationship evolved even as wild boar turned into pigs through a process of domestication that has been the subject of much debate. Underlying all interpretations of domestication, however, is the malleability of

SUS. HOGS.
1 S.Scrofa, var. Sinensis Wild Chinese H
2.   Capensis   Cape ―
3. Indicus   H. Babyrussa.
PHASCOCHŒRUS, ETHIOPIAN HOGS.
1.P.Alami   Aliani's H.
DICOTYLES.   PECCARIES.
1. D.torquatus   Collared P.
2. labiatus   White-lipped ―

suids, which gives them a wider range of possible relationships with humans than other domesticated animals. As a result, there are numerous ways to keep pigs for the production of meat – ranging from free-range husbandry to sty-reared, urban and industrial agriculture – and a concomitant variety of human–pig relationships as well.[3]

The domestication of wild boar into pigs was more similar to the transformation of wolves into dogs than of aurochs into bovines. The boar, in addition to being renowned as a courageous and fierce wild animal, is highly adaptable and omnivorous, capable of being a prey animal and finding benefit from proximity to humans. Accordingly, it is possible that both wolves and pigs in some sense 'chose' domestication, or at least were more integral to the process than earlier anthropocentric models that made domestication solely a matter of human agency.

A rendering of an Enteledont (*Dynohyus*), a large, ferocious and thankfully extinct pig-like omnivore often nicknamed 'Hell Pig' or 'Terminator Pig'.

Wild boar from the *Hunting Book of Gaston Phoebus, Comte de Foix*, early 15th century.

opposite: William MacGillivray, illustration of types of hogs, Plate XLII from *The Edinburgh Journal of Natural History, and of the Physical Sciences*, vol. I (1835–9).

It was the ubiquity of the omnivorous *Sus scrofa*, capable of devouring what humans eat and throw away, that made the wild boar so suitable for cohabitation and domestication. Yet we must also ask what was in it for the wild boar, as it is sheer hubris to imagine that humans forced domestication upon the wild pig. Because pigs are willing to move but do not need to be herded, only feed during some parts of the day, enjoy the company of each other and of other species, and are quite intelligent, perhaps domestication might best be seen as 'a treaty between consenting intelligent parties who entered into the agreement in a spirit of mutual self-interest'.[4] At least, of course, until slaughtering time.

Pigs changed physically under domestication and can quickly regress to wildness. This makes the distinction of pigs as 'wild' or 'domestic' a problematic one, as domestic pigs can fend for themselves, breed with wild boars and even start to look like wild boars. Wild-living pigs, a category that includes wild boar and feral pigs – which are biologically domestic but anthropologically and ecologically wild – are an increasing

Wild boar (*Sus scrofa*) female with suckling piglets.

problem in many parts of the world, a reminder of the irrepressible animality of pigs.[5]

Pigs were not really 'pigs', of course, until domestication, when traits necessary for survival in the wild, such as spots or stripes for camouflage, were lost. Domesticated pigs developed longer bodies, shorter legs and large, floppy ears, because pigs kept in captivity no longer needed to be quite so alert. Domesticated pigs also have a curly tail, one that contrasts markedly with the long, expressive tails of wild pigs. Today most commercially farmed pigs do not even get to keep the diminished tail that they have, as piglets have their tails docked after birth to prevent tail biting, a

'Le Cochon de Siam' and 'Le Sanglier', and from wild to domesticated: 'Le Marcassin' and 'Le Cochon de Lait', from the Comte de Buffon's *Histoire naturelle* (1799–1800).

common problem in the situations of stress and confinement that mark intensive hog farming.[6]

Archaeological evidence suggests that the pig was initially domesticated about 9,000 years ago simultaneously in Eastern Turkey and in China. The assumption was that after this initial domestication, pigs were transported through trade and human migration around the world.[7] Recent DNA studies, however, have made the case for the multiple local domestication of pigs. This work suggests that the first domesticated pigs in Europe had Near Eastern ancestry, confirming that some farmers migrated to Europe with their livestock. Pigs domesticated from European wild boar ancestry emerged later, reflecting a secondary domestication influenced by the newcomers. To make matters even more complicated, these European pigs then spread across the continent before replacing the original domestic pig of the Middle East.[8]

Pigs were significant to human development in regions where wild-living pigs were brought into human society. In China, home to half of the world's pig population, archeologists have found evidence of pig bones dating to 8000 BCE. Pigs were clearly being bred in China by 5000 BCE and became a significant food source.

A Han Dynasty Chinese model ox-cart carrying a sleeping pig in comfort; c. AD 25–220, earthenware.

White jade pig, tomb goods from Eastern Han dynasty China, AD 25–220.

'Siamese Breed', hand-coloured lithograph by Thomas Fairland from a drawing by William Nicholson after painting by William Shiels, from David Low, *The Breeds of the Domestic Animals of the British Islands* . . . (1842).

Pigs also had ritual significance in China, important both in the iconography of the Hongshan culture (4700–2900 BCE) and as symbols of prestige buried with the dead as ceramic and jade figures in the Han dynasty (206 BCE–220 CE). The pig (*hai*) remains associated with fertility and virility as the twelfth sign of the *sheng xiao*, or Chinese zodiac. In 2007 the Chinese government's family planning department expected a 20 per cent increase in births, as it is considered auspicious to have children during a Year of the Pig.[9]

Pigs in China were confined long before those in Europe, so they matured quickly and fattened easily, especially in comparison to those in Europe. These foraged in the woods surrounding villages before being fattened on beech mast and acorns in a practice known as 'pannage.'

Pigs remain important to the Chinese economy and culture, where pork remains the preferred meat and where millions of small, short, fat pigs are still being raised in millions of rural households. There are dozens of different breeds of pigs in

China given the country's ecological diversity, although there has been an increasing use of crosses with foreign breeds, a process that created controversy in the 1930s when reformers attempted to transform pigs and pig-breeding by importing American pigs and Western methods, replacing local knowledge and practices.[10]

This replacement of indigenous pig breeds by imports and hybrids is a dominant pattern in the modern global history of the pig, one marked by standardization and homogenization. Developments in Britain usefully illustrate the emergence of modern breeds and the concomitant decline in the genetic diversity of pigs. From before Roman occupation to the Middle Ages, English pigs were semi-wild, bristly animals that largely found their own sustenance in the woods. As the woods were

Chinese propaganda poster linking pigs and prosperity, 1960s.

Berkshire Breed' and 'Old English Breed', hand-coloured lithographs by Thomas Fairland from a drawing by William Nicholson after paintings by William Shiels, from David Low, *The Breeds of the Domestic Animals of the British Islands* (1842).

cut down for timber and charcoal the pig became an animal more likely to be fattened on cereals and legumes or kept as a 'cottage pig' and fed kitchen scraps. These Old English hogs, with substantial regional variation, dominated until the eighteenth and nineteenth centuries, when the rage for 'improvement' of domestic animals began. The standard English pig was crossed with imports from China to create a smaller pig that would grow rapidly. These suited farmers that raised young animals that were later driven to London in their thousands to be fattened on brewery and dairy wastes before being slaughtered.

Sketch of a Tamworth pig, 1880s.

The best known of these breeds was the Berkshire, described in 1825 as 'long and crooked snouted, the muzzle turning upwards; the ears large, heavy and inclined to be pendulous; the body long and thick, but not deep; the legs short, the bone large, and the size very great'.[11] Improvements of Berkshires and other breeds continued throughout the nineteenth century; these were charted in registries and demonstrated in the flesh at agricultural fairs. At the Royal Show in Birmingham in 1876 three kinds of pigs, Large, Middle and Small Whites (also known as Yorkshires) dominated.[12] Over time the Large White became the most important pig in the world, standing at the centre of the commercial pork industry, consigning many other heirloom and regional breeds to extinction or near-extinction in the process.

The National Pig Breeders Association, now known as the British Pig Association, was formed in 1884, partly in response to criticism from American buyers that English pigs were not breeding true to type. Today the British Pig Association recognizes twelve breeds – the Large and Middle Whites, the Tamworth, the Berkshire, British Saddlebacks, Chester Whites, Gloucester Old Spots, Hampshires, Durocs, the Landrace, Large Blacks and Welsh – although there are many other kinds of pigs in Britain and throughout the world, many of them now quite rare, due to the emphasis on breeds that rapidly produce high-quality pork. Several field guides exist for those interested in learning about different breeds of pigs, although it is increasingly rare for most people in the urbanized world to see any living pigs on a regular basis, much less a variety of breeds.[13]

The development of the modern pork industry is responsible for the long-term decline of both household pig raising and the number of pig breeds. In Russia and Eastern Europe, for example, pork was common meat for peasants, with many families keeping a pig or two each year to be fattened and consumed at Christmas or on other feast days. Given the overall poverty of peasants' diets, ownership of a pig or two was an important element in family survival, as it was for many households throughout the

'Neapolitan Breed', hand-coloured lithograph by Thomas Fairland from a drawing by William Nicholson after painting by William Shiels, from David Low, *The Breeds of the Domestic Animals of the British Islands* . . . (1842).

world. In the Soviet era, however, the population of indigenous pig breeds and the animals' genetic variation declined as the state took over production and worked to standardize the industry around the Russian Large White pig. This breed accounted for almost 90 per cent of all pigs in the Soviet Union in the 1980s, as pigs became livestock rather than backyard animals.[14]

A similar transformation took place in Latin America, where commercial agriculture and improved pigs followed rising income levels. Imported breeds now dominate commercial production in Mexico, Brazil, Argentina and Chile. Yet the small space that a pig can be kept in, along with their efficiency in creating meat from table scraps and surplus crops, means that pigs have remained a significant part of the lives of the poor. In Bolivia, for example, most pigs are still kept in villages, not on farms. The native pig, the black, long-haired Bolivian Criollo, serves as a form of currency, especially in rural areas. Unlike in Haiti, where the indigenous *kochon kreyol* were exterminated in the 1970s and '80s following American concerns about the possible spread of disease to US agribusiness, Bolivians have found that both production and profit could be increased by modifying the traditional system, not by importing pigs that would displace the Criollo.[15]

Throughout the globe, however, one pattern seems unmistakable: modernization and development have served both to distance humans from animals and to undermine the diversity of pigs themselves. While the creation of modern pig breeds has made it possible for so many people to imagine a similar-looking pig, it has also ended thousands of years of household and small-scale farming, a lived relation and shared history with pigs that gave those animals material and symbolic significance in a number of the world's cultures.

Gathering acorns for pig food, 'November' in the calendar section of *The Hours of Henry VIII*, an illuminated manuscript of c. 1500.

2 A Shared History

Pigs and humans have had a lengthy shared history, one that was not always marked by alienation. As wild boar and as domestic animals, pigs provided humans with food and proved good to think with as human societies developed. While pigs were central to some human environments and could be praised and celebrated, they were also sometimes marginalized and made subjects of ambivalence, if not faced with outright opprobrium.

In Melanesia, pigs have a high cultural profile and great symbolic significance. For the Kaulong people of Papua New Guinea, pigs are prestige items, physically and symbolically central to society. Pigs and humans are not seen as radically different from one another. Instead, humans and animals share activities that define them as either 'human' or 'inhuman', with pigs sometimes behaving like humans and humans sometimes behaving like pigs.[1] The sacrifice of pigs and distribution of pork serves to complete ceremonial displays and establishes personhood and respected status. As a result, raising pigs is a central activity for men and women, one that involves feeding, grooming and training. Bonding between human and pig is essential, as the pigs typically roam the bush during the day and return to their caretakers' huts at night. To help the pig bond to its human, a magical powdered lime is blown into the piglet's nostrils so it will forget its natural mother. In some

Keren Su, 'Portrait of a Huli Woman', Tari, Southern Highlands, Papua New Guinea.

26

instances, tiny unweaned piglets with low prospects for survival are nursed at a woman's breast, a tangible connection between human and pig that makes children and piglets siblings.[2]

The most valuable pig in Kaulong society is a 'tusker', a male whose upper canines have been removed, permitting the lower canines to grow full circle to reenter the lower jaw. Specialists are rewarded for this dental work, while the owner of a tusker will use spells and ceremonies to enhance the pig's growth and protect it from harm. Tuskers are ceremonially sacrificed and the tusks are made into an ornament that can be displayed in the mouth in tense intergroup situations, enabling the wearer to say to others, 'Watch out, I can be like a pig. I am powerful and dangerous.' All of the Kaulong's pigs are raised with the expectation that they will be ceremonially butchered and distributed as pork to people outside of their village. Sacrificial pigs are killed in the morning after an all-night song ceremony (*lut a yu*, 'singsings with pigs') tied to rites of passage such as a child's first tooth eruption, male initiation, female puberty,

A faience sow suckling piglets, emblem of Isis as the Great White Sow of Heliopolis, a symbol of motherhood, in ancient Egypt, Third Intermediate Period (1085–760 BCE).

marriage exchanges and burials. Singing begins at nightfall and often involves competition between groups. At dawn the pig is placed in the centre of the clearing and a visitor is asked to kill it. As the pig squeals, the host group sings to drown out the pig's death cries. After butchering, no owner or caretaker will consume his or her own pig. Instead, the visitors take portions of the meat back to their own villages.[3]

Pigs have remained central to social and ceremonial life in Melanesia even after missionization and modernization. Pig ownership and pig killing continue to convey status, wealth and power. In Vanuatu pigs have been used symbolically by modern statesmen to build political capital, promote their personal authority and express community solidarity and national unity at times of political and cultural transition, linking pre-contact traditions to contemporary politics. Curved pig tusks feature prominently on the Vanuatu flag and currency and the national beer is called Tuskers. In 2006 Vanuatu was declared 'the world's happiest nation', perhaps because important chiefs and powerful men and women share their wealth, including pigs, with the people.[4]

In contrast to the long-standing centrality of the pig in Melanesian cultures, in ancient Egypt pigs became materially and symbolically marginalized. The drainage of swamps for grain and livestock production made the control of pigs a priority and contributed to their decline. Because of the relative ease with which households and communities raised pigs for food, pigs and pig-keeping came to represent and embody individuality and community autonomy, leading to a crackdown by emerging regimes.[5] While pigs were once a symbol of Lower Egypt, the region centred on the Nile Delta, consolidation of political authority by Upper Egypt (c. 3000 BCE) saw pigs relegated to a symbol of evil and treachery associated with Seth, the murderer of Osiris and the enemy of Horus. As swine became less desirable as livestock and as symbols, their status further declined; they were first avoided, and then made subject to limited prohibition and taboo. The food taboo that is part of the value system of pastoral and nomadic Jews and Arabs thus has its political, cultural and ecological roots in Egypt.[6]

In Jewish law pork is one of a number of foods (known as *treif*, 'non-kosher') that it is forbidden to consume. Leviticus 11:7–8 and Deuteronomy 14:8 mark swine as unclean, and the philosopher Maimonides argued in the twelfth century that such dietary laws were important to keep the body healthy. While he acknowledged that pork does not appear to be harmful, he argued that pigs were filthy animals and thus worthy of prohibition. The cultural anthropologist Marvin Harris has argued for the ecological roots of this prohibition, noting that pigs tend to eat foods that are also perfect for human consumption, potentially bringing them into competition with people. Pigs also required water and shady woods, conditions that became increasingly scarce in the Middle East.[7]

The Muslim prohibition on pork consumption derives from the Qur'an and ultimately from Judaism. Most Muslims rarely

Artemis having sent a monstrous boar by to ravage the Greek region of Calydonia, the Calydonian Hunt was mustered to kill it. The hero Mealeager is doing so on this 3rd-century Roman marble sarcophagus from Vicovaro.

A pig on a Roman tile.

encounter pigs unless they live among non-Muslims who keep them, which has often engendered conflict between Muslims and Christians. Where wild-living pigs pose a problem in the Islamic world, Christian hunters are generally used. This tension forms the plot of Iranian playwright Gholam-Hossein Sa'edi's *The Stick-Wielders of Varazil* (1965), where an Armenian Christian is called upon to save a rural village from the predations of boars.[8]

Boars and domesticated pigs were important material and symbolic animals in classical antiquity. Pigs were an important food in ancient Greece, as they were economical to raise, easy to sell and good to eat at both family dinners and temple feasts. Because of their similarities to humans – Aristotle called pigs 'the animals most like people' – pigs also had ritual uses: piglets were sacrificed to the gods and men swore oaths on boar testicles. Pigs were especially associated with Demeter, the goddess of fertility and agriculture.[9]

Pigs remained an important food in the Roman Empire, where they were ritually sacrificed in state religion and private cults. They made their first appearance in Greco-Roman mythology when, as prophesied, Aeneas sacrificed a white sow and her litter of thirty piglets to Juno, stilling the Tiber river and enabling the Trojans to row upstream. Both wild boars and domestic pigs

The sacrifice of a pig to Ceres was an important ritual marking the start of the harvest season. Roman, 1st century BC.

Aeneas meets the prophesying sow in a 2nd-century Roman marble relief. The reference is to a prophesy in Virgil's *Aeneid* that Aeneas would find a sow under an oak tree when he arrived at the future site of Rome.

appear in Roman life and art. Wealthy Romans kept boars in their private parks (*vivaria*) to be hunted, killed and served on special occasions. Boar-hunting was a popular pastime, depicted and celebrated in reliefs, sculpture and on coins. In addition to hunting scenes one can find images of the sacrifice of pigs raised on farms to the gods, often as part of the *suovetaurilia* involving a pig, sheep and bull.[10]

Ambivalence about the similarity of pigs and humans and debates over human and animal natures appear in the legend of Circe's transformation of Odysseus' followers into pigs, told in Homer's *Odyssey* and Ovid's *Metamorphoses* and frequently depicted by artists. In Plutarch's *Gryllus*, however, Circe tells Odysseus that to return his companions to human form would be 'a disaster'. Odysseus disagrees, so Circe makes it possible for him to speak to one of the pigs to try to persuade him that it is better to be human. Gryllus, a pig, remarks: 'now you come and try to persuade us, who have all the good things we want, to give them all up . . . and to sail away with you, reverting again to the condition of man, the most miserable thing alive.' Positing animal existence as superior, Gryllus argues

The slaughter of a pig in a detail from the stele of Cornelius Successus, a Roman, Abruzzo, Italy.

A follower of Odysseus turned into a swine by Circe in an illustration on a vase depicting a scene from *The Odyssey*, 5th century BC.

that 'animals have souls that are more naturally and perfectly disposed to produce virtue than men have'.[11]

Pliny the Elder's *Natural History* contains more practical ideas about pigs, ranging from the obvious (they 'love to wallow in dirt and mire') to the culturally specific (swine whose tails curl to the right-hand side are 'more likely to appease the gods in sacrifice'). He had no doubt about the intelligence of pigs, telling stories about hogs so well trained by their swineherds that they could walk themselves to market and wild boars that knew how to cover their own tracks. Yet swine were first and foremost a food, and Pliny's account concludes with a paean to

An anonymous engraving of the Prodigal Son from *Speculum Humanae Salvationis* (1496).

pork, especially sow liver foie gras, made by feeding the pig dry figs and mead.[12]

Ambivalence about the pig became a hallmark of Christianity. On the one hand, an association with pigs could distinguish Christians from Jews. On the other, the pig represented all that was unclean and disgusting.[13] The most important New Testament appearance of pigs occurs in the parable of the Prodigal Son, where Jesus told of a young man who suffered the indignity of becoming a swineherd when he recklessly lost his father's inheritance. Jesus also cast demons into a herd of pigs, the Gadarene swine, which caused them to stampede over a cliff. By transferring 'unclean spirits' into pigs, the animals were further stigmatized, strengthening a negative association with pigs that has persisted.[14]

Even a religious figure known for his love of animals and humility before nature, St Francis of Assisi, disapproved of pigs. When a newborn lamb was attacked and killed by a sow at the monastery of San Verecondo, Francis was reminded of the

Albrecht Dürer, *The Prodigal Son*, 1496, engraving. The Prodigal Son finally comes to his senses amid the pigs he has been forced to look after.

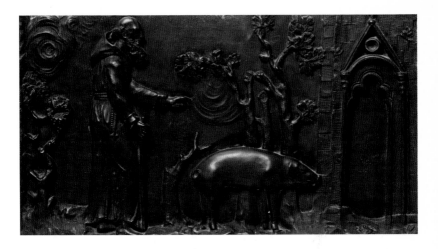

sacrifice of the Lamb of God and cursed the sow for the murder, saying: 'Alas, brother lamb, innocent animal, you represent Christ to men. A curse on that impious beast that killed you; may no man or beast ever eat of her.' The sow became sick and died after three days of agony. Her carcass was thrown into the moat so that the meat would be untouched.[15]

An early 19th-century French cast-iron charcuterie sign depicting St Francis of Assisi.

An association with pigs was used to bestialize and dehumanize others, especially Jews. Christians drew upon the Jewish prohibition on the consumption of pork to promote anti-Semitism. In late medieval Germany, a condemned Jew had to be led to execution wrapped in the skin of a pig, and in some executions victims were hanged upside down alongside pigs that were also hung by their rear legs. In Dannelbourg, France, the reenactment of the killing of Judas was accompanied by the sprinkling of pigs' blood. The most infamous iconography linking Jews and pigs was the *Judensau*, a derogatory and dehumanizing image of Jews in contact with unclean and non-kosher pigs. These images became popular in the thirteenth century and appeared in woodcuts and as sculptures and carvings in churches. Many of these images show Jews suckling from a pig and eating its excrement. In the sixteenth century these images proved useful in depictions of heresy. An anti-Jesuit print of 1569 portrayed Pope Paul IV as a disgusting sow, one that copulated with a dog to give birth to Jesuit swine. A 1545 German print depicted the Pope holding steaming shit in his hands and riding on the back of a sow.[16] Much later, *Judensau* was used as term of insult by the Nazis, showing the enduring usefulness of the pig as a symbolic instrument of dehumanization. As Boria Sax has observed, 'Those who wished to brutalize and slaughter other people . . . would find it psychologically easier if they thought of their victims as swine.'[17]

Sometimes pigs themselves were killed to help people make sense of their often chaotic world. There were at least 37 prosecutions of swine between the ninth and nineteenth centuries, with pigs accounting for half of all recorded animal executions in medieval Europe.[18] In 1266, at Fontenay-aux-Roses near Paris, a pig convicted of having eaten a child was publicly burned by

Woodcut of a *Judensau*, a dehumanizing image of Jews suckling from a sow and eating its excrement, c. 1470.

order of the monks of Sainte-Geneviève. In 1379 a herd of pigs trampled the son of a swine-keeper, throwing him to the ground and fatally injuring him. The entire herd was arrested as accomplices and sentenced by the court to death. Not wanting to endure the loss of the swine, a friar sent a petition to the Duke of Burgundy asking that all of the pigs, save for four animals, be pardoned. The others were set free to later become food for the community. Finally, a sow was condemned for murder in Senlis in 1567 after devouring a four-month-old girl. The sow was hanged from a tree, perhaps offering a small degree of consolation to the family and the community by helping them

Butchering a pig, a scene familiar throughout the world's cultures, depicted here in a 14th-century stained-glass window in St Mark's church, Bilton, Warwickshire.

'make sense of certain seemingly inexplicable events by redefining them as crimes'.[19]

Today, when most criminal justice systems hold that non-human animals lack moral agency, these trials and executions seem bizarre evidence of the superstitions of an earlier time. They remind us, however, of the depth of the entanglement of pigs and humans in history, the closeness and intimacy, for better or worse, of this relationship. Then and now, of course, most pigs end up as pork. Traditions of killing and eating pigs throughout the world, however, were profoundly transformed in the nineteenth and twentieth centuries, especially in the United States, where an intensification of the transformation of pigs into pork took place.

3 Hogs in the New World

Many of the elements of modern meat production first came together in the United States, where there was no indigenous wild species of pig (the pig-like javelina of the southwest is a peccary and cannot be domesticated). From the arrival of pigs in the new world with the Columbian Exchange – the exchange of plants, animals, people and ideas between the Eastern and Western hemispheres – through the emergence of modern meatpacking in the cities of Cincinnati and Chicago, many important developments in the dominant human–pig relationship – in which the former kill and consume the latter – took place in America, although with different implications for different regions and social groups.

With their omnivorous diet and rapid reproduction, pigs were excellent partners in European colonization. As Alfred W. Crosby famously noted, 'one who watched the Caribbean islands from outer space during the years from 1492 to 1550 or so might have surmised that the object of the game going on there was to replace the people with pigs, dogs and cattle'. As part of the Columbian Exchange, native peoples were decimated by European diseases, while the population of animals left by Columbus and his followers exploded on the rich grasses and wild fruits (and the absence of predators) of the 'new world'.[1]

Like the European explorers and colonists they accompanied, pigs had multiple points of arrival. Columbus brought eight pigs to Cuba in 1493 and other Spanish explorers left pigs on other islands to provide food for future visitors. Pigs proliferated rapidly in their new homes. In 1514 Diego Velásquez de Cuéllar wrote to King Ferdinand II that the pigs he had brought to Cuba had increased in number to approximately 30,000, or 'more pigs than I ever saw before in my life'. Hernando de Soto brought thirteen pigs with him to Florida in 1539 and had 700 at the time of his death in 1542. Because pigs needed little care and could forage for themselves, pork was the predominant meat for early explorers and colonists. Most of them liked it: a visitor to Brazil wrote in 1601, 'The swine doe like very well here and they beginne to have great multitudes, and here it is the best flesh of all.'[2]

There was plenty for omnivorous pigs to eat in the new world, which is why their numbers exploded so dramatically. Three sows were brought to Jamestown, Virginia in 1607, resulting in more than 60 pigs in eighteen months.[3] Robert Beverly

A François Delpech print of soldiers attempting to commandeer someone else's pig for provisions, c. 1820.

noted that there were so many pigs in Virginia in the late seventeenth century that they did 'swarm like Vermaine upon the Earth' and were so numerous that they were left out of inventories of an individual's wealth. Beverly noted that 'The Hogs run where they list and find their own Support in the Woods without any Care of the Owners.' These pigs quickly reverted to a more feral type, with long legs, narrow backs and sharp tusks. Their appearance and personality led them to earn the name 'razorback' in America and in Australia, both colonial situations where settlers relied upon pork as their primary meat. Like North America, New Zealand proved 'a swinish paradise', soon full of wild pigs descended from those left by Captain Cook and still called 'Cookers'. Pigs were particularly important for the Maori, providing them with their first large land animal, one that produced ample protein and fat for consumption and sale.[4]

Despite the centrality of pork to colonial diets, pigs were more often the subjects of complaints than praise. Swine were such a nuisance in Massachusetts that as early as 1633 the court declared, 'it shall be lawfull for any man to kill any swine that comes into his corne'. Colonists thought it was fine for hogs to fatten themselves in the woods, but not on English fields. In 1635 animal pounds were created where wayward swine could be held, but in 1636 the problem had become so bad that it was legal 'for any man to take them, either alive or dead, as hee may' if swine were not restrained. This law gave half the value of the animal to the finder and half to the colony, resulting in protests that led to the repeal of the law two years later. The agency of pigs caused more conflict between colonists than any other animal, ones that often fell along class lines, as pigs were favoured by poorer colonists while wealthier ones had both more cattle and more fields to be rooted up.[5]

Pigs also created significant conflict with Native Americans, for they competed with them for shellfish and destroyed their crops and stores. Roger Williams, the founder of Rhode Island, described how 'the English swine dig and root these Clams wheresoever they come, and watch the low water (as the Indian women do)'. He added that 'Of all English Cattell, the Swine (as also because of their filthy dispositions) are most hateful to all Natives, and they call them filthy cut throats.' Ringing and yoking of hogs was practised to protect fields and prevent rooting, although the emphasis was always upon protecting English property and sentiments.[6]

Pigs were an important food and trade item in the maturing British North American colonies. By the time of the revolution, Americans had plenty of pigs for domestic consumption. The Virginian planter William Byrd II negatively associated the residents of backcountry North Carolina with their swine, noting that they lived 'so much upon swine's flesh' that it deformed their physical features and made them 'extremely hoggish in their temper, and many of them seem to grunt rather than speak in their ordinary conversation'.[7] The colonies and, after independence, the American states also developed a growing trade in salted, barrelled pork, much of which was shipped throughout the Caribbean. During the War of 1812 a businessman named Samuel Wilson provided the army with pork in barrels. These were labelled 'US' for the United States, but people began joking that they stood for 'Uncle Sam', which quickly became a personification of the government.[8]

In the early nineteenth century a key shift in hog management occurred when new livestock laws redefined the purpose of fences, which were now supposed to keep pigs in, not out. Such laws were quite unpopular, as many Americans were used to letting their pigs run free to find their own sustenance. The

Bill Payne driving hogs through town, Black River Falls, Wisconsin, early 20th century.

resulting 'hog wars' in states like Delaware pitted poor farm families who believed in the 'privilege of the range' against landowners who wanted to protect improvements to their property. Laws ultimately required that pigs be penned (if not, they could be shot on sight by anyone or kept and sold at public market, with the rightful owner able to redeem his animal by paying a fine), marking the triumph of private property interests over customary grazing privileges.[9]

As Americans spread west in the nineteenth century, their pigs went with them, although they were generally left to fend for themselves in the woods before being rounded up for slaughter. While small farmers processed pork locally, drovers moved thousands of hogs to the north and the east where colder winters were more conducive to preserving meat. Hog-driving season ran from mid-October to mid-December. Drovers moved hogs eight to ten miles per day before stopping at one of the

The disassembly line in action: a 'Panoramic Picture Illustrating the Pork Industry', c. 1900.

many 'hog hotels' along the route that provided lodging and food for the drivers and pens and corn for the hogs. So many hogs moved through Knoxville, Tennessee that an observer noted that it seemed that 'all the world were hogs and all the hogs of the world had been gathered there'.[10]

In an era marked by poor but improving infrastructure, pigs were used as a means of transporting corn on the hoof. As Oliver Johnson recalled of pioneer life in Indiana, 'settlers wasn't long in findin' out that feedin' hogs and drivin' them to these river markets was a good way to sell their corn'. Johnson took part in drives of hundreds of hogs in Indiana, managed by a boss on horseback and six to eight men who went on foot, with a wagon following to pick up hogs that 'gave out'. So many hogs were transported on foot to Cincinnati that the *Brookville American* complained in 1834 that 'for the last three weeks our eyes have been greeted with scarce any thing, except *vast droves of the swinish multitude* . . . all winding their way to Cincinnati'.[11]

Developments in Cincinnati in the first half of the nineteenth century created the modern pork industry. Located on the Ohio

46

Serial Rel panorama picture illustrating the pork industry 1900

river, Cincinnati was perfectly situated to become the centre of American pork production. By the 1830s more than 100,000 hogs were processed annually in the city. By the start of the Civil War the number had risen to over 400,000 and the city was widely known as 'Porkopolis'. Cincinnati's pork producers were merchants, not farmers, investing in live hogs that could be sold as bacon, ham and lard many months later. In contrast to today's highly concentrated pork industry, Cincinnati's producers were decentralized, with over 70 firms slaughtering or curing meat in 1864.[12] Entrepreneurs in Cincinnati pioneered the use of mass-production techniques in their famous 'disassembly line' that turned pigs into pork. Companies in the city literally used 'everything but the squeal', including the fat and grease, which were rendered by entrepreneurs including William Proctor and James Gamble into commercial products like soap.[13]

Travellers to Cincinnati inevitably commented on the new world of animal industry they saw there. The amazed account of Frederick Law Olmsted in 1857 is worth quoting at length:

We entered an immense low-ceiled room and followed a vista of dead swine, upon their backs, their paws stretching mutely toward heaven. Walking down to the vanishing point, we found there a sort of human chopping-machine where the hogs were converted into commercial pork. A plank table, two men to lift and turn, two to wield the cleavers, were its component parts. No iron cog-wheels could work with more regular motion. Plump falls the hog upon the table, chop, chop; chop, chop; chop, chop, fall the cleavers. All is over. But, before you can say so, plump, chop, chop; chop, chop; chop, chop, sounds again. There is no pause for admiration. By a skilled sleight of hand, hams, shoulders, clear, mess, and prime fly off, each squarely cut to its own place, where attendants, aided by trucks and dumb-waiters, dispatch each to its separate destiny – the ham for Mexico, its loin for Bordeaux. Amazed beyond all expectation at the celerity, we took out our watches and counted thirty-five seconds, from the moment when one hog touched the table until the

next occupied its place. The number of blows required I regret we did not count. The vast slaughter-yards we took occasion not to visit, satisfied at seeing the rivers of blood that flowed from them.[14]

Although the pork industry built Cincinnati, not all residents approved of this situation. Upon moving to the city, Frances Trollope learned that household 'slops' were to be thrown into the streets, where 'the pigs soon take them off'. Free-roaming pigs scavenged the garbage and cleaned the streets in most American cities in the nineteenth century, although they also proved quite the nuisance. As Frances Trollope wrote in *The Domestic Manners of the Americans* (1832),

It seems hardly fair to quarrel with a place because its staple commodity is not pretty, but I am sure I would have liked Cincinnati much better if the people had not dealt so very largely in hogs! The immense quantity of business done in this line would hardly be believed by those

overleaf:
Pork packing in Cincinnati: killing, cutting, rendering, salting, 1873.

49

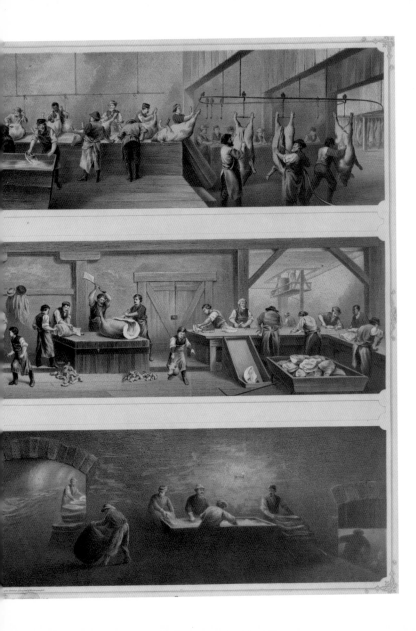

who had not witnessed it ... If I determined upon a walk up Main Street, the chances were five hundred to one against my reaching the shady side without brushing by a snout or two, fresh dripping from the kennel.[15]

Thanks to the railroads, the technology of 'ice' packing and the centralizing forces unleashed by the Civil War, a regional and national pork manufacturing industry developed. In the space of one generation pork packing lay increasingly in the hands of a small number of manufacturers, including Chicago's Philip

4

As poor Jemmy Jumps
With his fine new turn'd Pumps,
Was strutting so pleas'd with his dash;
A great Hog in the street,
Took him off both his feet,
And threw pretty Jemmy down splash.

Pigs as urban
nuisances,
New York, early
19th century.

Armour, an entrepreneur who entered the business during the war, making a huge profit by providing pork to the Union army. Starting in the 1880s modern manufacturers emerged, almost totally wiping out the traditional merchants. With the advent of modern transportation and refrigeration, Chicago became the nation's pork-producing centre, serving as 'hog butcher for the world'. Unlike in Cincinnati, where processors were scattered throughout the city, the post-Civil War meat processing industry in Chicago was centralized, located on the south side of town at the famous Union Stockyards, separating the production of meat from urban life. Visitors to Cincinnati were shocked at the number of pigs they encountered while in the city, whereas in Chicago the stockyards themselves became a tourist destination.[16]

The ubiquity of pigs in American cities and towns was noted by travellers and promoted class conflict. Pigs were important players in urban ecologies and subsistence strategies as well as a public nuisance. New York City, in particular, struggled to deal with its free-roaming pig problem, passing a series of ordinances (most of which failed) starting in the seventeenth century. In the nineteenth century pigs were increasingly seen as undermining efforts to improve the city. An 1817 law that declared that any pig running loose in the streets could be taken to a public pound engendered substantial controversy. In the protests that followed, the pig was described by its defenders as 'our best scavenger' and street cleaner and was also praised for providing cheap food for the poor in winter. The law was criticized for producing a 'swarm of informers' who would prey 'on the defenceless poor'.

Under a subsequent law, two men were charged with the common law misdemeanour of 'keeping and permitting to run

A pig-shaped flask incised with railroad routes, produced by the Kirkpatrick brothers of Anna, Illinois, c. 1881.

'Pull My Tail and Hear Me Squeal', advertising card for Chicago's Nelson Morris & Co., Packers and Lard Refiners.

hogs at large in the city of New York'. One of the accused pleaded no contest to keeping 'about forty hogs' at his place and was given a small fine. The other defendant, a butcher named Christian Harriet, fought the case, leading to an 1819 trial. The district attorney argued that 'hogs running in the streets are a nuisance, that they attack children even, and do various other mischief', which included copulation and defecation in front of ladies. The defence argued that the attack on pigs was a war on the poor, asserting that 'a great convenience, and almost an essential source on the score of provisions would be taken from the poor or less opulent of the citizens by a conviction'. They added that while 'the dandies, who are too delicate to endure the sight, or even the idea of so odious a creature, might exult', many 'poor families might experience far different sensations, and be driven to beggary or the Alms House'. The elite triumphed, however, as Harriet was convicted and a new principle – that pigs in the street constituted a public nuisance – was permanently established. Despite revisions to the laws and much contest of the regulations by New Yorkers who believed that keeping pigs in the streets was their right, little was done actually to remove pigs from them. When it did happen, the council received petitions from those whose pigs were confiscated for the return or their hogs or the monetary equivalent. Even an effort to slaughter confiscated pigs to give meat to the poor failed, since this law was ruled unconstitutional because it took property from individuals without compensation. As a result, it proved much harder to get rid of pigs in practice than in theory.[17]

Foreign travellers continued to comment on the prevalence of pigs in the streets of New York City. On his American travels in 1842 Charles Dickens observed that 'Two portly sows are trotting behind this carriage, and a select party of half-a-dozen

A half-mile of pork at Armour's great packing-house, Chicago; half of a stereographic photograph of 1899.

gentlemen-hogs have just now turned the corner.' In the wake of the 1849 cholera epidemic the city began a more effective crackdown, although this effort largely pushed the pig population further north. By the late 1850s, when Frederick Law Olmsted was planning Central Park, he found the land above 59th Street 'steeped in overflow and mush of pig sties, slaughter houses and bone boiling works, and the stench was sickening'.[18] In 1859 the anti-pig crusade culminated in an attack on piggeries in the area known as Hog Town (between 50th and 59th Streets from Fifth to Eighth Avenues). Over 3,000 hogs were captured in this raid and many hog pens were destroyed, with the paradoxical but predictable effect that the city had to spend more money on the removal of offal and garbage than before. By 1860 pigs were removed to north of 86th Street and the era of free-ranging hogs, at least in New York City, was over.[19]

Free-roaming hogs in New York and elsewhere were important elements in the subsistence strategies of the working

Removing pigs from the city: 'The Police, Under the Direction of Inspector Downing, Clearing the Piggeries of Bernard Riley', New York City, 1859.

classes. In the American South hogs were similarly crucial in enabling rural southerners to develop and maintain an independent way of life. Prior to the Civil War, the South raised two-thirds of America's hogs, most on the open range, which enabled yeoman farmers to let hogs run free. As was once common in the rest of the nation, farmers would capture their hogs at the end of the year, saving some for slaughter and driving others to market.

The Civil War, however, proved especially devastating to Southern hog farmers. By 1880 the former Confederate States produced 2.6 million fewer hogs than they had in 1860. After the Civil War farmers found themselves increasingly tied to a national commodity-crop economy and faced the collapse of the open range, which was legislated out of existence in the early twentieth century. Although the US Department of Agriculture worked to teach Southern farmers how to raise pigs in pens, the economy of scale promoted the development of larger and larger operations that undermined important community traditions, such as winter's hog-killing days.[20]

William Gedney,
Man Feeding Hogs,
Kentucky, 1972.

Hog-killing days were important community occasions, providing the first taste of fresh meat and the promise of more
meat throughout the winter. The traditional Southern way of
raising and slaughtering hogs and preparing pork would have
been familiar to earlier generations of Americans and, for that
matter, to rural communities throughout the world. Hogs were
killed, cut up, cured and smoked at home, typically in late
November or early December, once the weather turned cold
enough to keep the meat from spoiling. Folklore tied the time of
slaughter to phases of the moon. As one man put it, 'We'd kill

Slaughtering
pigs in winter;
a calendar illus-
tration from
an illuminated
manuscript of
c. 1500.

hogs on th' full moon, or just about th' full moon. While th'
moon was shrinkin', th' meat'd shrink. There'd be a lot'a lard
an' grease if it 'uz on th' shrinkin' of th' moon.' On the appointed
day, scalding water was readied, either in a large cast-iron bowl
built in a furnace or in an oil drum. The hog was killed; its throat
was slit, and after bleeding out, it was dragged to the scalding
pit to loosen the hair. The hog was scraped, then the hamstring
was exposed on both hind legs and a gambling stick was slipped
behind the tendons so the hog could be strung up for gutting
and cleaning. Entrails, organs and fat were prepared and cooked
right away – as with cracklin's, souse meat and headcheese – or
set aside to make sausage. Hams, shoulders and 'middling meat'
(side meat) were most commonly cured at the smokehouse.[21]

Everyone seemed to have their own family recipe for curing
and smoking pork, something reflected in the regional variations of hams in the American South. Many country hams were
salt-cured, aged and sold in rough cotton bags. The most famous
branded Southern ham – better known as a country ham – was
the Smithfield ham, produced from pigs that grazed in the
peanut fields of Virginia and North Carolina after the harvest.
These hams were dry-cured, smoked over a hickory fire, then

rubbed with molasses and black pepper and hung to dry for at least a year. A country ham is necessary to make red-eye gravy, which is done by adding water (or coffee) to country ham pan drippings and cooking it down.[22]

While red-eye gravy can still be found in the South, the rituals that laid the foundation for the Southern appreciation of pork

Farmers scraping the bristles off a hog after slaughtering and scalding, France, 1908.

Preparing a pig's head for the table in France in the 1930s.

have largely disappeared. Instead, nostalgic scenes of tradition-al hog killing have become a staple in Southern letters. Ferrol Sams of Fayette County, Georgia, recalled in his autobiographi-cal novel *Run with the Horsemen* that 'one of the events that made school attendance almost unthinkable to the boy was hog-killing. This involved so much planning, organization, expertise, and total group participation that the boy likened it to feudal preparations for a siege. The frantic activity and excitement were exhilarating, and the boy was attracted to it primarily because so much of the ritual horrified and repelled him.'[23] In *A Childhood*, Harry Crews observed how 'farm families swapped labor at hog-killing time just as they swapped labor to put in tobacco or pick cotton. Early one morning our tenant farmers, mama, my brother, and I walked the half mile to Uncle Alton's place to help put a year's worth of meat in the smokehouse. Later his family would come and help us do the same thing. Before it was over, everything on the hog would have been used.' Hog-killing days were literally imprinted on Crews, who was badly burned after accidentally being tossed into the scald-ing pot while playing a game of 'pop the whip' with other kids.[24]

Also significant, and now largely absent from the human–pig relationship, was the sense of appreciation of the pigs for providing humans with pork. North Carolinian Belinda Jelliffee recalled her reaction to the scene: 'Oh! The shrill frightened squeals they made! A sound accusing, asking for help, full of consummate awareness of annihilation! The completely unbearable fact that every pig was a member of the family.'[25] Today there are few independent family farmers and small slaughterhouse operators left in the American South, although the pig remains both a staple and a symbol of Southern culture, as evidenced by the countless signs featuring pigs that denote barbecue joints in my native Georgia and elsewhere. Because it is increasingly rare to see a living pig and because people are so disconnected from their meat, the Old South Farm Museum in Woodland, Georgia, holds an annual hog-killing that includes lessons in butchering, curing and chitlin-making. In 2008 more than 400 people registered, mainly families interested in showing their kids the old ways and educating them about the source of their food.[26]

Slaughtering a pig, from a marginal decoration to an illuminated manuscript, c. 1470–80.

The different experiences of pork production in the North and South highlight the range of human–pig relationships and their rapid transformation in the past several centuries. The Southern folkways surrounding pigs and their slaughter are a reminder of a more intimate and engaged way of living with pigs, one once common throughout the world. Laments about the loss of tradition and the degradation of the human–pig relationship, while occurring at different times in different places, mark the arrival of modern, intensive means of producing meat.

4 Meat

Pork is the most widely eaten meat in the world, with nearly 100 million metric tons consumed worldwide in 2006. Roughly half of the world's pork is consumed in China, where urbanization and rising incomes are continuing to drive pork consumption upwards. The nations with the highest per capita consumption of pork are in Europe, with Denmark, Germany, Spain and Poland leading the way. In the United States pork ranks third in annual meat consumption, behind beef and chicken, but the average American still eats 23 kg (51 lb) of pork per year, the majority of it processed as bacon, lunchmeats, hot dogs, sausage and ham.[1] Many people are either unaware or in denial about how all of this meat is produced, perhaps only thinking, as that everyman Homer Simpson did, that such a delicious bounty could only come from a 'wonderful, magical animal'. In reality, however, pigs are killed by their millions for their meat, much of which is produced in an industry that, in the words of Michael Pollan, 'offers a nightmarish glimpse of what capitalism can look like in the absence of moral or regulatory constraint'.[2]

A hog carcass is divided into seven primal cuts: the leg (produces ham), loin (source of chops, back ribs, Canadian bacon and tenderloin), side pork (bacon), spare ribs (ribs and salt pork), Boston shoulder (pork steaks, Boston roasts and shoulder roll), picnic shoulder (roasts and steaks as well as ground

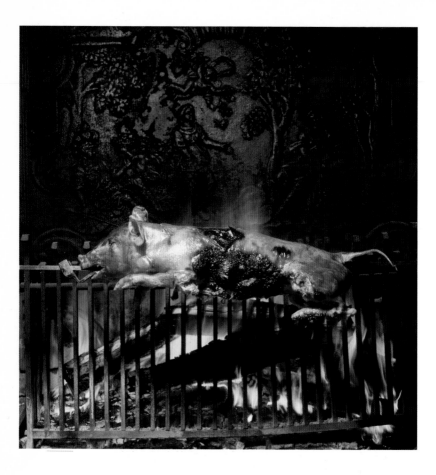

Roasting a suckling pig (a piglet slaughtered between the ages of two and six weeks).

pork and sausage) and jowl (can be sliced like bacon or cured for seasoning meat). Different groups have consumed different cuts of pork over time, making pork consumption a useful lens into race, region and class. In the United States, lower-income households consume more pork products than middle- and high-income Americans. African Americans tend to consume more pork, 6.25 kg (14 lb) more per person annually, than whites. Pork consumption, like pork production, is highest in the Midwest and in the South.[3]

Pork consumption is also an index of change over time. Although per capita pork consumption is predicted to fall in the United States with the growth of the elderly and Hispanic populations, pork was once the dominant American meat. Pork consumption was so prevalent in nineteenth-century America that Dr John S. Wilson of Columbus, Georgia, observed in 1860,

Cuts of pork, 1930, with commentary on national, regional and racial preferences for different parts of the pig.

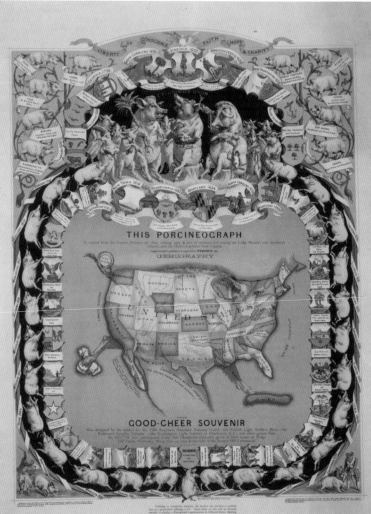

'the United States of America might properly be called the great Hog-eating Confederacy, or the Republic of Porkdom'. He noted, 'so far as meat is concerned, it is fat bacon and pork, fat bacon and pork only, and that continually morning, noon, and night, for all classes, sexes, ages, and conditions'. In addition, 'hogs' lard is the very oil that moves the machinery of life'.[4]

The type of pork Americans ate was, like the slaughter of pigs, tied to the seasons. In the autumn and winter hogs would be slaughtered and cured and fresh pork either roasted or stewed. Preserved pork, either cured or brined, was eaten throughout the year, often used as a seasoning for other kinds of dishes. Americans were unlikely to eat fresh pork in the summer, as it was 'considered to be exceedingly unwholesome during the months of high temperature'.[5]

The pork Americans ate was a marker of social class. Salt pork in a barrel, along with bacon, was a poor family's meat, while elites preferred cured hams and fresh roasts. The industrialization of pork packing in Cincinnati and Chicago led to greater standardization of cuts of meat and the creation of different varieties of barrel pork. But by the turn of the twentieth century, barrel pork faded away, as consumers increasingly preferred (and could afford) bacon and ham.[6]

Traditionally, hams and bacon were dry-cured with sugar, salt, smoke and saltpetre, which helped give the meat some colour. These techniques took time and were not easily adaptable to large-scale production, so packing firms switched to wet-cure methods, using new ingredients like borax and boric acid to inhibit bacterial growth. The publication of Upton Sinclair's *The Jungle* (1906) raised concerns about the effects of borax on human health and led to federal regulation of the meat industry. After the Department of Agriculture banned all meat additives except 'common salt, sugar, wood smoke, vinegar, pure

Salt pork in the proverbial pork-barrel, 2008.

spices, and, pending further inquiry, saltpeter', the industry developed the use of sodium nitrate and nitrate, which were introduced to the meat by 'vein pumping' them through the animal's circulatory system. These innovations reduced curing times for hams from about ninety days to five, although they produced a softer, sweeter and blander product, especially compared to hams produced the old-fashioned way.[7]

Bacon originally left the packers in 1.8–4.5-kg (4–10-lb) slabs. The marketing of sliced and wrapped bacon helped to expand demand for bacon in the 1920s, creating a more convenient product for consumers. By the mid-1960s more than 60 per cent of American families regularly purchased bacon, a meat that had been successfully 'upscaled'. American bacon comes from the pig's belly and contains significant streaks of fat. It can be produced in a matter of hours in a modern pork-processing plant. British bacon is made from the meat on the back of the pig and is traditionally given the 'Wiltshire Cure': soaked in a unique brine mixture under refrigeration for four to seven days. The county of Wiltshire, where pigs were raised on pannage in Pewsham Forest, became a major pork-producing region in England. Its centrality persisted thanks to its thriving dairy industry; Daniel Defoe wrote that 'bacon is raised in such quantities here, by reason of the great dairies, the hogs being fed with the vast quantity of whey, and skim'd milk, which so many farmers have to spare, and which must otherwise be thrown away'.[8] In the United States, bacon cured in this way is often called Canadian bacon, and what is called a 'rasher' in Britain is called a 'slice' or a 'strip'.

Ham and bacon are made from whole pieces of the pig, but, as the aphorism goes, pork processors use 'everything but the squeal'. An important mechanism for using meat from different parts of the animal is sausage, which is traditionally packed in

'Drawing his own conclusion': a British postcard of a pig pulling a plate of sausage for Marsh & Baxter's, sausage-makers.

the animal's intestines, known as casings. Although sausage-making was a part of traditional butchering, commercial meat processing led to the standardization of sausage varieties, categorized by how they were cured. Fresh sausage was intended for immediate consumption. Lightly cured and cooked sausage could be kept for a few days or weeks, while 'summer sausage' was dried and smoked so it could be kept for months.

The hot dog appeared in the late nineteenth century, based on traditions from Frankfurt or Vienna (hence the terms frankfurters or wieners). These sausages contained finely chopped meat (primarily pork and beef) and were cured with salt and chemicals before being cased, smoked and precooked so they would be ready to eat. By the 1920s the hot dog was a fixture in American popular culture, tied to places of public leisure (such as Coney Island) and entertainment (especially baseball games). Hot dogs were, and remain, a democratic food item, as they are inexpensive and easy to prepare and eat. To produce hot dogs more quickly, pork processors needed to liquefy meat

A tin of Spam.

to completely mechanize the production process. The Swift company demonstrated the key technological breakthrough at the 1939 World's Fair: a machine that turned meat into a semi-liquid batter that could be moved through the stages of production along conveyor belts. This new 'continuous flow' of meat, fat, cereal filler, flavourings and preservatives into artificial casings was perfected in 1960's Frank-O-Matic, which was so automated that it required almost no workers. Emulsified meat went in one end and completely ready hot dogs came out the other, having been injected into artificial casings, smoked and cooked.

The mechanization of hot dog and sausage manufacturing was devastating to female packinghouse workers, who lost jobs by the thousands. People also began to wonder what was in these convenient foods. In 1969 Ralph Nader attacked the hot dog as a type of food intended to 'defraud' the consumer by selling 'substandard meat palatably'. While such complaints irritated the industry, they were indeed using hot dogs to sell less desirable animal parts in a re-created package. Each day more than 50 million hot dogs are eaten in the United States, an average of 80 per person per year.[9]

By the 1960s pork was 'an entirely different meat than it had been a century before', transformed by consumer demand and, more significantly, industry innovations. Salt pork, especially in barrels, had disappeared, replaced by pre-sliced bacon, and Americans increasingly consumed fresh pork and new varieties of convenient meat.[10] One final form of convenient pork – Spam – merits discussion, in part for its contributions to culture. Hormel Foods introduced this well known, if regularly disdained, canned pork product in 1937 under the name Hormel Spiced Ham. While today the company claims 'Spam is just that. Spam', many vernacular acronyms have been created for the product, including 'Stuff, Pork, and Ham' and 'Something Posing As Meat'. Actually, Spam products contain chopped pork shoulder meat with ham meat added, along with salt, water, sugar and sodium nitrate. You can now buy Spam products in a number of flavours.

Because it does not need refrigeration, Spam became infamous during the Second World War, when American soldiers ate it regularly. These soldiers spread Spam throughout the Pacific Theatre and today the most Spam per capita is consumed in Hawaii and the US territories of Guam and the Mariana Islands. In the USA Spam has long been associated with the lower class and with hard times. Hormel Foods has exported Spam to 41 countries. It was tremendously popular in the United Kingdom in the 1940s, when the United States shipped Spam as part of the billions of dollars' worth of supplies sent to wartime Britain. Although spam fritters are now hard to find in fish-and-chip shops, the food product did lend its name to the colloquialism 'Spam valley' (referring to places where residents appear wealthy but in fact are living at poverty levels) and to an infamous Monty Python skit of 1970, where Spam appeared in every meal at a café and a group of Vikings sing 'Spam, lovely Spam, wonderful Spam'. Junk e-mail is labelled 'spam' because, like these Viking songsters, it overwhelms other dialogue. The food item is celebrated every July in Austin, Minnesota, where Hormel Foods has its headquarters, and where one can visit the official Spam Museum, and at the annual Waikiki Spam Jam street festival in Hawaii.[11]

F. A. Pazandak, 'Swine on Highland Farm', North Dakota c. 1910–19.

The creation of more convenient meat went hand-in-hand with changes to the farm and to pigs. In traditional hog farming, pigs were raised seasonally on farms that typically gave the animals access to the outdoors and enabled interaction between them and their environment. After the Second World War this relationship was severed, following the model of intensive chicken production. Improved feeds, antibiotics, confinement systems and the separation of the hog-raising process along different stages in pig growth resulted in larger and leaner animals that could be brought to market sooner. Vertical integration, in which companies in the supply chain were united through common owners, and contract farming further standardized the industry, which now presides over an ever more efficient – some would say terrifyingly efficient – conversion of animals into meat.[12]

Modern consumers tend to know very little about how their food is produced. In the early twentieth century Upton Sinclair observed that the origins of our meat are 'no more than the universe to be questioned or understood'. In addition to forcing changes to the American meat industry, *The Jungle* exposed the costs, both physical and philosophical, of 'pork-making by machinery, pork-making by applied mathematics. And yet', Sinclair wrote, 'somehow the most matter-of-fact person could not help thinking of the hogs . . . One could not stand and watch very long without becoming philosophical, without beginning to deal in symbols and similes, and hear the hog-squeal of the universe.'[13]

Sinclair witnessed important developments to the pork 'disassembly line' pioneered in Cincinnati. Entrepreneurs figured out how to use more and more of the pig and to process the parts more 'scientifically'. Windsor Leland invented the 'slaughtering machine' in Chicago in 1866, which first hooked a still-living pig, hauled it up to an elevated conveyor belt, and

Pig heads for sale at a French market.

carried it to where its throat was cut. It was then 'shaved, scraped, scalded, gutted, quartered, sectioned and subdivided into various cuts'.[14] Advances in transportation, including the invention of refrigerated railroad cars and commercial trucks, and innovations in financing, including futures contracts, where people agree to buy a particular amount and quality of pigs and pork at a specified price, aided in the growth and consolidation of a national meat industry which extended its reach into individual homes. On the retail side, butcher shops were increasingly replaced by supermarkets, a self-service development heralded by Charles Saunders, who opened the first Piggly Wiggly store in Memphis, Tennessee, in 1916. He took the name from an analogy he drew between the way piglets rushed to their sow and the way shoppers swarmed clerks at a general store.[15]

In the 1950s the American Secretary of Agriculture, Ezra Taft Benson, told farmers to 'Get big or get out'. Government subsidies and relaxed regulation enabled the meat industry to consolidate and grow rapidly. While the modern slaughterhouse perfected the disassembly line, it was not until the 1980s that pig farmers applied assembly line principles to the hog farm. Under the direction of Joseph Luter III, whose grandfather had founded Smithfield Packing Company in Virginia in 1936, Smithfield Foods began to raise its own hogs in pursuit of 'total vertical integration', in which the company would control every stage of production, from piglet to pork products. Farmers in this new system had to become contract workers for Smithfield, which owned all the pigs and provided the feed and antibiotics. Many hog farmers were driven out of business or left the industry. Where there were more than 650,000 hog farms in the United States in the late 1970s, there were fewer than 70,000 in 2004. By 1999 Smithfield was America's largest pork producer, killing more than a quarter of all the pigs sold. The top four American pork packers now control an estimated two-thirds of total pork production, with Smithfield alone killing and processing 27 million hogs in 2005, producing 6 billion pounds of packaged pork.[16]

Control over nature through the practice of artificial insemination has been central to the growth and consolidation of the industry. In 1990 only 7 per cent of American swine-breeding involved artificial insemination. Today more than 90 per cent of farms use this technology. They do so to create more uniform pigs and to avoid bringing a prize boar into contact with sows, because modern pigs are remarkably susceptible to disease as a result of the close quarters they share. In 1991 Smithfield purchased the US rights for the genetic lines of pigs improved by Britain's National Pig Development Company. These hogs more efficiently converted feed to protein and developed little fat, resulting in meat that was substantially leaner than most pork, something that appealed to American consumers, who were moving away from fatty meats and toward lean meats like chicken. As a result, in 1986 the National Pork Board began rebranding the pig as 'the other white meat', a marketing campaign that led to improved sales of pork. Today's pigs are bred lean, kept in heated and ventilated confinement barns, for 'keeping pigs at just the right temperature allows them to devote every ounce of energy to one purpose: growth'.[17]

This 'chickenification of the American pig' is seen as a great triumph by the industry and, indirectly, by the public, which has become used to inexpensive and lean pork. While a growing number of writers and critics have highlighted the hidden costs of American meat, in many instances, that is all they can look for, as the pigs and other animals raised in concentrated animal feeding operations (CAFOs) are largely invisible. In addition to transforming the lives of pigs for the worse, this model has also fundamentally transformed the way farmers look at their animals. Where once a farmer knew and paid attention to individual pigs, now the health and efficiency of the overall herd is what matters.[18]

With fewer farmers raising more pigs, many traditional hog-producing regions of the United States have been transformed. Iowa, which led the United States in pig production since the 1880s, has seen its number of farms with pigs decline 83 per cent in the last 30 years. As of 2002, half of all the Iowa pigs sold were raised under a contracting arrangement. Pigs were once known as 'mortgage lifters' and the odour of pigs was 'the smell of money', but confinement operations are increasingly viewed negatively and many Iowans have to visit the Des Moines Zoo to see pigs. One casualty of the decline of family farms is the

tradition of the Pork Queen, in which teenage girls compete to be chosen as ambassadors for county or state pork producers based on their attractiveness, personality and knowledge of pigs and the pork industry. Where once twenty states had Pork Queens who competed for a national title, today only one state – Iowa – has them.[19]

Hog-farming was also way of life in the American South, but now there are few independent family farmers and small slaughterhouse operators left. More than 200,000 farmers were driven out of the business in the South between 1974 and 1991, and in Georgia, where there were almost 2.4 million hogs in 1979, there were only 345,000 in 2002, most raised indoors in confinement systems. [20] The exception to this trend is North Carolina, where Smithfield's Tar Heel packing plant is the world's largest hog-processing facility, slaughtering up to 32,000 hogs per day. North Carolina is now the number two hog-producing state in the country, although not without controversy, centred on the effects of concentrated operations on animals, workers, the environment and rural communities.[21]

These transformations in the United States have been mirrored throughout the world, albeit at different times and scales. The intensification and globalization of the pork industry has led to the disappearance of smaller pig farms in many countries. For example, in 1998 Australia had about 3,000 producers with an average herd of 97.5 sows, a marked consolidation from the 50,000 producers with three or four sows in the 1960s. In Europe, herds are growing in Spain, Denmark, Belgium and France, but are declining in the Netherlands, Germany and the UK, in part due to environmental regulations. In 1999 Smithfield Foods bought a controlling stake in the Polish company Animex, announcing that they hoped to make Poland the 'Iowa of Europe'.[22]

In Mexico pressure from American exports of both live hogs and pork products have promoted greater consolidation of the pork industry. In South America, Brazil remains the largest producer and exporter of pork due to its low labour and feed costs. In Vietnam, where pork is a mainstay of the diet and pigs are culturally significant as an indicator of prosperity, the government, working with the Australian Centre for International Agricultural Research, has worked to import pig breeds, in particular the genetic lines of Yorkshire pigs, to improve the nation's stock. This initiative has resulted in the production of heavier but leaner pigs, although many local breeds are disappearing as a result.[23]

China is the world's largest producer and consumer of pork. Since the founding of the People's Republic of China in 1949 there have been many models for raising pigs. Private pig ownership was abolished and then promoted several times before the 1970s, when a 'household contract responsibility system' gave farmers greater power and thus more enthusiasm for raising pigs. The creation of free markets for pigs in the 1980s helped fuel the development of the Chinese pork industry, one increasingly marked by specialization, industrialization and large-scale operations. Today, however, approximately three-quarters of all pigs are still produced in rural households. These pigs tend to be smaller and fattier than those raised in state-run or private farms, with their more intensive production and better genetics and management. Because pork consumption is growing along with urbanization and rising living standards, China is a net meat-importing country, one where backyard production and small slaughterhouse operations are seen as an obstacle to greater herd uniformity, disease control and food safety.[24]

These concerns are global ones, as the remarkable success of the pork industry in improving the efficiency of pigs has come

with a price, and not just the one paid by pigs. Pork in the USA became so lean that meatpackers have had to inject saline marinades into the meat before sale and restaurants have had to smother pork in heavy sauces. Many cooks claim that modern industrially produced pork is less tasty than it used to be and the industry largely concedes this point, as pork can be too acidic, resulting in a condition known as PSE ('pale soft exudative') meat. Much of America's best pork is exported to Japan, where buyers choose the meat by colour (darker pork has less acid and more flavour). American consumers get 'the other white meat' along with a less satisfying eating experience.[25]

The creation of PSE pork has been found to be related to stress: anxious pigs live with their muscles immersed in lactic acid, making their meat go bad. Industry scientists discovered that in selecting for lean, fast-growing pigs, geneticists had also selected a gene that made hogs prone to panic. Despite the removal of the PSE gene from most breeding stock, the problem of poor-quality pork has persisted, indicating that something else is making pigs undergo stress. That something, of course, might just be 'the modern pig's monotonous life in cramped quarters'.[26]

It turns out that if workers physically touch pigs, let them out of their crates for walks and give them things to play with, their stress levels go down. But this degree of interaction with pigs, not to mention the space required, is no longer possible in large-scale hog farming. Instead, breeders and producers are hoping for more technological fixes, breeding 'better' pigs that 'can stand on a 2´ × 7´ rectangle of concrete all their lives without going lame or insane with boredom'. As Nathanael Johnson concludes, 'bit by bit scientific breakthroughs have emancipated the hog industry from the demands of nature, but each freedom comes at a price. Each new liberty for pork producers depends on further control, further domination of the pig'.[27]

A farmer carrying his pig near Kunming, China, 1982.

Profits also depend on further exploitation of the human labourers in the pork industry, especially at the slaughterhouse, where skilled manual labour is required to run the 'disassembly line'. Packers have struggled to find technological ways to replace the skilled hand labour required to bone, skin and cut pork. In fact, because the cutting of hams was highly skilled labour, these men were often the best-paid workers in modern meatpacking. Other positions, however, were allocated along racial and gender lines. Men dominated in both the slaughtering process and in the cutting and trimming positions. White women ran the sliced bacon packaging operations, which were often open to public view on tours. This association of white 'American' women with bacon production contributed to its 'upscaling' in the 1920s. In the 1950s the United Packinghouse Workers of America (UPWA) successfully opened this area of meatpacking to black women, without any negative consequences, as American consumers were more interested in the ease of using sliced bacon than worrying about who put it in packages.[28]

The modern pork-packing plant is increasingly dependent on minority and immigrant workers, and the turnover rate in these factories often reaches 100 per cent. Charlie LeDuff, who worked undercover at a Smithfield plant in North Carolina, wrote that 'Slaughtering swine is repetitive, brutish work . . . Five thousand quit and five thousand are hired every year. You hear people say, "They don't kill pigs in the plant, they kill people".' Employees are also at risk at large-scale hog-raising operations, where pig shit and its fumes can incapacitate and kill farm workers.[29]

Broader concerns have been expressed about the environmental impacts of these concentrated animal feeding operations (CAFOS). A large operation with 50,000 pigs produces 227,000 kg (500,000 lb) of pig urine and excrement every day. By 1995 pigs in North Carolina – the second largest pork producing state in the USA – were producing 19 million tons of waste per year, 2.5 tons for every citizen in the state. That summer, an eight-acre waste 'lagoon' burst, releasing 25 million gallons (95 million litres) of liquid waste into the New River, killing thousands of fish and polluting the river for sixteen miles. The half a million pigs at a Smithfield farm in Utah generate more shit than the inhabitants of Manhattan, part of a total discharge of waste from Smithfield Foods of 26 million tons per year. If hog farmers had to treat their waste as municipalities do, they would lose so much money they would be driven out of business.[30]

In addition to the problem of waste, hog farms also produce a foul smell. This odour problem has generated local opposition to large-scale pig production, resulting in a trend toward situating large hog-feeding operations in remote, sparsely populated areas, including Milford Valley, Utah, the Texas Panhandle area, the eastern plains of Colorado and North Dakota and the prairie provinces of Canada. Pig production is thus increasingly removed from where the resource base and infrastructure has been traditionally located.[31]

The pork industry has made great progress in its conquest of nature, but their victory over the pig will always be incomplete, a fact that an industry analyst admitted pleased him in a conversation with me at the National Pork Forum about the inability of farmers to overcome seasonal fluctuations in breeding. The industry's greatest potential enemy, however, is the whim of consumers, who have always preferred convenience and low prices, but increasingly seem worried about both food safety and the welfare of the animals in this industrial system of food production.

In addition to having to deal with campaigns and protests by both organized and individual animal welfare and animal rights activists and critics of industrial agriculture, the pork industry has had to respond to a counter-revolution (actually, a return to tradition) that has followed in the wake of its success. Consumer interest in both better-tasting pork and animal welfare has led to growth in niche pork producers. These producers, such as the Niman Ranch Pork Company, are 'trying to adapt to who the pig is', rather than forcing the pig into an efficiency-based system. Niman Ranch pigs graze in pasture and root at the earth. They are produced naturally, not via artificial insemination, and need no antibiotics. Even though Niman Ranch pork costs more, they currently are unable to find enough producers to raise pigs according to their protocols to meet consumer demand.[32]

Much of the American interest in niche pork is tied to the slow food movement and the rediscovery of traditional food-ways in Europe. American food critics and aficionados celebrate the Ibérico pig from southwestern Spain. These pigs, fed on

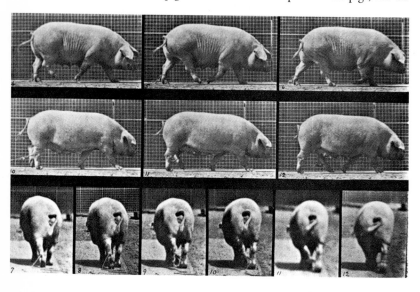

The rationalization of nature: Eadweard Muybridge's motion study photographs of a sow walking, plate 674 from *Animal Locomotion* (1887).

Beating acorns out of a tree to feed pigs in winter; a calendar illustration from an illuminated manuscript of *c.* 1500.

acorns in the wooded meadowlands known as the *dehesa*, produce meat that is dark, red and finely striated with fat. Even better, this fat is monounsaturated, the kind that is healthier and produces complex flavours and aromas. *Jamón ibérico de bellota*, produced from pigs fed exclusively on acorns and herbs, is said to literally melt in your mouth. Ibérico hams are treated like fine wines and are very expensive (a typical 100g tasting plate of finely-sliced ibérico in Spain would cost €20, and the hams imported to the United States can cost as much as $1,000 each), confirming the criticism that consuming food that is both tastier and better for humans and animals is a class privilege.[33]

American hopes for their own Ibérico are placed on the Ossabaw Island pig, a descendant of the pigs the Spanish let loose on the islands of the southeast coast of North America. The pigs that survived on this Georgia coastal island are rare, and their pork is heavily marbled, making them a delicacy. Another rare breed of pig of interest to 'foodies' is the Mangalica, a curly-coated pig from Hungary that is fatty and hardy. This breed nearly disappeared as the public expressed a preference for leaner meat and

the Hungarian government subsidized different breeds. There were just 198 Mangalica pigs left in 1991, but today there are about 50,000, all raised in a traditional manner. Most of the meat is shipped to Spain, where it is processed in a manner similar to *jamón ibérico*. The rescue of this endangered breed has also helped revitalize traditional agriculture in Hungary, where the Mangalica was known for producing excellent salami and lard.[34]

A growing number of households are moving towards self-sufficiency by keeping livestock, including pigs. While chickens dominate the 'urban farming' movement, pigs can be kept provided one has enough space (experts recommend at least a 9 × 9 m (30 × 30 foot) yard), tolerant neighbours and the proper permits. The Tamworth breed is often recommended for backyard farmers, for a feeder pig purchased at a weight of 18 kg (40 lb) will reach full-growth and a butchering weight of 91 kg (200 lb) in about five months. Both backyard and small farmers in the United States currently face a shortage of slaughterhouses to process their meat, as local, family-owned operations closed in

A man checks Iberian hams hanging in a drying room at the Embutidos y Jamones Fermin farm in La Alberca near Salamanca.

Heritage breed Ossabaw Island Hogs at the National Colonial Farm, Accokeek, Maryland.

the face of stricter health controls and the consolidation of the pork industry.[35]

Household pig-keeping ended in Britain and the United States in the face of sanitary laws, new leisure activities and the rise of factory production, all of which contributed to the expanding distance between humans and pigs. Yet concerns about industrial agriculture have led to calls for a return to household pig-keeping. The British journalist James Buchan has argued that raising household hogs could 'emancipate us from the supermarket economy, and such of its baleful consequences as low or lowish wages, poor husbandry, poor animal welfare, agricultural subsidies, crap architecture on the bypass, motor traffic and general *malbouffe*'. He adds: 'To buy two pigs as weaners, build them up as stores, fatten them as porkers and baconers, put them in a trailer and then drive them to the butcher forces one to witness the consequences of one's actions.'[36]

A French greeting card promoting good luck in the New Year, *c.* 1905.

In addition to raising their own pigs and restoring nearly extinct breeds, some are working to re-create artisanal pork traditions in the USA. In downtown Seattle, Armandino Batali makes, sells and serves culatello, prosciutto, salami and soppressata at his restaurant Salumi. Batali produces 1,350 kg (2,500 lb) of cured meat per month, with the pork coming from white-hoofed Berkshire hogs raised in Kansas, where they are free to root and range as they like on a 1,500-acre spread. The meat, free of hormones, additives and water injections and marked by large amounts of marbled, intramuscular fat, has attained mythic status among American foodies.[37]

The popularity of Salumi is part of a renewed interest in pigs and pork in the American culinary community. Numerous websites (including the 'Bacon of the Month Club') and blogs promote local varieties of bacon and ham, several restaurants specialize in pigs and pork (including Cochon in New Orleans), and several pork-based cookbooks, including Stephane Reynaud's *Pork and Sons* (which won the Grand Prix de la Gastronomie Francaise in 2005) and Martin Picard's *Au Pied de Cochon – The Album* (drawn from his Montreal restaurant), have become bestsellers. Pork has been so newsworthy in recent years that one writer has called this a 'porcine renaissance', one marked by chocolate-bacon candy bars, pork cocktails and chefs with pig- and pork-related tattoos.[38]

Perhaps the iconic moment in this explosion of interest in alternative pork takes place in Michael Pollan's bestseller *The Omnivore's Dilemma: A Natural History of Four Meals* (2006), where he caps off his meal 'prepared entirely from ingredients I had hunted, gathered, and grown myself' with a wild pig he shoots in California. The hard-earned yet satisfying 'transcendently slow' meal that results is contrasted with his fast-food meal at McDonald's (home, incidentally, of the pressed pork

McRib sandwich, available only occasionally as a 'limited edition' menu item), one representing knowledge of and engagement with the world, the other representing ignorance, most notably in the way that the true costs of industrial agriculture are occluded.[39]

Factory farming has also been the subject of political action, most notably in legal attacks on the ways in which pigs and other animals are confined. In modern farrowing systems, sows are kept in 'gestation crates', steel stalls so narrow that the pigs cannot turn around. This practice, which the industry defends as necessary to limit fighting between breeding sows, has been successfully challenged in recent years. The European Union's scientific veterinary advisory committee found that these gestation crates had 'major disadvantages' for animal welfare, concluding that 'sows should preferably be kept in groups'. The European Union passed a law phasing out sow crates by 2012. In the meantime, both Britain and Sweden have already acted to ban sow stalls.[40]

In November 2006 voters in Arizona approved Proposition 204, the Humane Treatment of Farm Animals Act, which banned sow gestation crates and veal stalls, by a wide margin. The pork industry seemed stunned at their defeat, despite an expensive campaign that argued, 'Proposition 204 is Hogwash'. Industry representatives unsuccessfully tried to depict this initiative as a radical animal rights action, but in fact the belief that farm animals should be able to stand and turn around is quite mainstream, seen in the passage of California's Proposition 2 (the Prevention of Farm Animal Cruelty Act, which prohibited veal crates, battery cages and sow gestation crates) in 2008 and in plans for similar voter-led initiatives elsewhere.[41]

Much of the industry could see the writing on the wall, for at the 2007 Pork Industry Forum a Smithfield vice-president spoke about the need to promote Corporate Social Responsibility (css) and announced plans to get rid of gestation crates and work to capture methane to stop pollution and slow global warming. The global meat industry will continue to have to deal with the consequences of their tremendous success in converting pigs to pork with greater efficiency and lower costs to consumers on a planet where meat consumption will only increase. Despite growing interest in alternative ways of raising pigs for pork, it is likely that fewer people will encounter living pigs in the future, much less have a direct, cross-species relationship with these remarkable animals.

5 Human–Pig Partnerships

While pigs are generally raised for slaughter as meat, pigs and humans work together at times. These partnerships are designed to take advantage of the pig's special skills, such as its keen sense of smell or its exceptional intelligence. People have long appreciated the 'sagacity' of the pig, and they have recently been shown to have episodic memory – remembering the what, when and where of a previously experienced event. For those who understand and wish to harness what the minister Henry Ward Beecher called the 'reasoning power of pigs', a remarkable partnership can develop.[1] Pigs and humans can, it seems, get along, through work and play, although the rising medical use of pigs, itself predicated on the numerous similarities between human and pig anatomy, offers some darker prospects.

One of the most well-known and long-standing human–pig partnerships involves the procurement of truffles. Sows have been used for generations to sniff out these fungi, which grow below the ground in association with tree roots, typically oaks. Scientists have discovered that truffles contain an irresistible pheromone, the same one that is synthesized in the testes of boars and secreted into their saliva when courting. This pheromone attracts the sow to the truffle and perhaps accounts for the reputation of truffles as an aphrodisiac. Pigs are naturally fond of truffles, but they do need to be trained to procure them.

A young pig selected because of its sensitivity to the smell of truffles is taught to walk on a leash and given a reward of corn kernels, pieces of potatoes or other treats by his master as he harvests the truffle.

Truffle-hunting dates back to Roman times, and the scarcity of truffles compared to demand has made them, in the words of the pioneering gastronome Jean-Anthelme Brillat-Savarin, the 'diamond of the kitchen'. The most desirable of the many edible truffles are the black truffle from the Périgord region of France and the white truffle from Italy's Piedmont. The town of Alba is at the centre of the Italian truffle industry and culture. Alba white truffles are harvested between September and December, and thousands are drawn to the annual truffle festival and auction in October. In part because of the tremendous value of these truffles (they routinely sell for thousands of dollars per pound; a Macau casino owner paid a record price of us $330,000 for a 3.3 lb white truffle in 2007), they are increasingly sniffed out by dogs, who, unlike pigs, have no interest in eating the delicacy.[2]

Pig and keeper looking for truffles in the Quercy region of France.

A variation on the image of a man and his pig searching for truffles provided great amusement to the hunting classes of nineteenth-century England. A gamekeeper trained a black sow as a pointer in the New Forest, figuring that having broken many dogs as stubborn as pigs he could do the same with the real animal. This pig hunted game alongside the dogs and was later exhibited in hunting demonstrations to amuse the owner's friends. Despite these skills, which were depicted in both hunting and husbandry literature over the years, 'she died the usual death of a Pig, and was converted into bacon'.[3]

An interesting effort to take advantage of the pig's desire to root and its strong sense of smell is taking place in Israel, where animal trainer Giva Zin is working to train pigs to detect land-mines. Zin has trained his pigs to find the mine and then sit down, although some of the time the pigs have accidentally detonated the mines (a training version, not a high explosive, thankfully) with their snouts. He is hoping to demonstrate the demining abilities of pigs, something more useful in other parts of the world than Israel, where suicide bombing is a more common threat than landmines. Elsewhere there might also be a greater willingness to use pigs, for as Zin reminds us, 'Jews don't like pigs. Even Jews who are not religious have a strong aversion to pigs.' But because there is no religious prohibition against looking at pigs or touching them, Zin hopes that Israeli attitudes about this use of pigs will change. As he concludes, 'I believe that even God likes my idea because I am using the pig for a good reason. Maybe in the future, after pigs have been used successfully in other regions, or after research confirms that pigs can be used for demining, Israelis will accept them for use on their own land.'[4]

Pigs have also worked with people in numerous animal acts that have attracted crowds through the centuries. In a common circus act, a clown dressed as a woman carries a baby in a blanket. When the baby cries, it is given a huge bottle of milk, which it quickly drinks. The audience is surprised and delighted to realize that the baby is in fact a piglet. The humour and delight comes from the cuteness of the piglet, which squeals, drinks and, for the most laughs, urinates on the clown or, even better, on another circus performer.[5]

The blurring of boundaries between humans and animals helps to account for the tremendous popularity of performances of 'learned pigs', which amazed and amused audiences by spelling, solving mathematical problems and answering questions by picking up cards placed upon the floor. In the late eighteenth century the learned pig proved a sensation in London. An illustration accompanying the sheet music for a popular song

THE WONDERFUL PIG. *Publish'd by I.V. Jones N.3 Piccadilly April 12. 1785.*

Thomas Rowlandson, *The Wonderful Pig*, 1785, etching. Over the chimneypiece is a placard, 'The Surprising PIG well versed in all Languages, perfect Arethmatician Mathematician & Composer of Musick'.

singing the praises of 'The Wonderful Pig' depicted one member of the audience thinking 'I should like it for a Tithe Pig', while the proprietor smugly acknowledges, 'I have brought my Pig to a fine Market.' Although it seems like virtually everyone knew of the performances of the learned pig, not all approved. The poet Robert Southey lamented that the learned pig was 'a far greater object of admiration to the English nation than ever was Sir Isaac Newton', while in Sarah Trimmer's *A History of the Robins*, an enlightened mother tells a group of children, 'though I was in London at the time he was exhibited, and heard continually of this wonderful Pig from persons of my acquaintance I never went to see him; for I am fully persuaded that great cruelty must have been exercised in teaching him things so foreign to his nature.'[6]

Concerns about the cruelty to animals that it was believed was necessary to create this animal act were addressed by William Frederick Pinchbeck, an automaton maker, magician and animal trainer from England who achieved great, if fleeting, fame in the United States. Pinchbeck faced American audiences sceptical that his 'Pig of Knowledge' was a living animal and concerned about the propriety of his performances. The numerous advertisements for his 'grunting professor' in American newspapers in the 1790s testify to both his originality and skill as a showman and animal trainer and the challenges of making a living in popular culture.[7]

Pinchbeck explained the mystery behind the learned pig's education in his book *The Expositor, or Many Mysteries Unravelled* (1805). Rather than starving or beating the pig, as was assumed by many of his critics, Pinchbeck used behavioural reinforcement to train the animal to pick up the correct cards imprinted with letters or numbers. The key to this process was the signal between the human and the animal when the pig reaches the correct card. Pinchbeck suggested that 'snuffing the nose' at the proper moment worked best, although over time he argued that

Frontispiece to *The Life and Adventures of Toby, the sapient pig: with his opinions on men and manners. Written by himself* (c. 1817).

one could remove the signal, for 'the animal is so sagacious that he will appear to read your thoughts. The position that you stand in . . . [that] will naturally arise from your anxiety, will determine the card to your pupil.'[8]

Pinchbeck's explanation of the mechanism behind the learned pig, along with overexposure of this animal act, cooled fervour for them in America for a while. In fact, it appears that the transatlantic public had tired of learned pigs, for they all but vanished for the next twenty years until Toby the Sapient Pig and his contemporaries became a sensation in London in 1817.[9] In 1835, in the wake of another round of popular educated pig exhibitions, Thomas Hood's verses on 'The Lament of Toby, The Learned Pig' imagined the pig's perspective on this animal act. In it, Toby asks, 'Why are pigs made scholars of?' Ultimately, however, even he realizes that 'public fame's unstable, / So I must turn a pig again / And fatten for the table'.[10]

In America learned pigs were popular before the Civil War, when performer Dan Rice exhibited his learned pig named Sybil, and in the late nineteenth century, when performing pigs appeared in sideshows and as part of the Barnum & Bailey Circus, where pigs were depicted on an 1898 poster ringing bells, playing cards, and making music on xylophones.[11] While to my knowledge no one has exhibited a learned pig or pig orchestra for years, marking yet another way pigs have disappeared from everyday life, performing pigs remain staples of carnivals, fairs and roadside attractions. The most famous of these attractions in the United States was Ralph the Swimming Pig, who performed at Aquarena Springs in San Marcos, Texas from 1969 until February 1996. Literally hundreds of pigs played 'Ralph' over the years until a local university purchased the park and converted it to educational uses. There was simply no place for a performing pig when the focus of Aquarena Springs shifted from entertainment to environmental preservation. Another diving and swimming pig act, Randall's High Diving Pig Show, was criticized after one of the pigs, 'Big Red', was accidentally electrocuted at a show in Austin, Texas, in 2005. People for the Ethical Treatment of Animals (PETA)'s position is that 'forcing pigs to dive or jump into water from heights is both cruel and dangerous'.[12]

Yet other types of pig-based entertainment seem to be flourishing in the USA, especially on the fairground circuit. The 'top hog' in the business is Valentine's Performing Pigs. Steve and Priscilla Valentine have performed thousands of shows at fairs

'Troupe of Very Remarkable Trained Pigs', Barnum & Bailey Circus Poster, 1898.

and sporting events and have a website where you can watch videos of their potbellied pigs in action on both David Letterman's and Jay Leno's late night television programmes. Their star performer is Nellie, whom they describe as the 'World's Smartest Pig!' Their pigs dance and jump, ride skateboards, play basketball and go bowling, among other feats.[13]

Performing pigs face their greatest competition from racing pigs, a show in which four small pigs race around an oval track hoping to be the first to get a treat, which, when I went to the pig races at the World Pork Expo in Des Moines, Iowa, was an Oreo cookie. A former Ringling trapeze artist named Roger Defoce has been training piglets for races since 1997 and does shows under the name Rosie's Racing and Performing Pigs. There are many other groups that will put on a pig race, including Hedrick's, All-Alaskan, and Robinson's, which accounts for the ubiquity of pig races at American state and county fairs.[14]

Extremely large pigs are another popular attraction at fairgrounds. The production and display of fat pigs emerged alongside efforts to improve breeds in the late eighteenth and early nineteenth centuries. In Britain these exceedingly fat pigs became

Ralph the swimming pig, Aquarena Springs, Texas. Many different pigs named Ralph entertained visitors to Aquarena Springs from the 1960s to the 1990s.

a fashion, with the animals entered into competition at agricultural shows (where judges were explicitly instructed 'not to
take into consideration the present value to the butcher of
the animals exhibited') and commemorated in numerous (and
charming) portraits and engravings. These pigs were often so
fat that they had trouble breathing and walking, although they
proved tremendous attractions. One writer noted that 'nothing
draws such a crowd of Yorkshire folk as a monster pig show', and
some giant pigs, such as the famous Yorkshire Hog that belonged
to Joseph Hudson, which weighed 610 kg (1,344 lb), brought in
nearly £3,000 in admissions between 1807 and 1809.[15]

American state and county fairs typically feature a special
enclosure featuring the area's biggest pig. The largest pig in
the United States in recent years was Big Norm, who weighed

Pig racing in
Sydney, Australia.

HUMORS OF THE AGRICULTURAL FAIR.

The Prize Pig welcomed home.

The Pig which gained no Prize welcomed home.

A MYSTERY EXPLAINED.

Farmer Smith.—"But how does he get along? He's too fat to walk."

Farmer Jones.—"Why he's a Propeller—Don't you see the screw at the starn!"

726 kg (1,600 lb) and lived in Hubbardsville, New York. The Guinness Book of Records believes that a Poland-China pig named Big Bill who died in 1933 is the largest pig ever, weighing 1,157 kg (2,552 lb).[16]

These gigantic pigs served to advertise a breeder's prowess and skill, thus making them mascots for their farms. Other pigs have served as literal mascots. During the First World War, Tirpitz the pig was one of the only survivors of the sinking of the German cruiser sms *Dresden*. Plucked from the waters off

Portsmouth on 14 May 1915, the pig became the mascot of HMS *Glasgow*, one of the ships that had destroyed his previous home. The pig was eventually retired to the Whale Island gunnery school in Portsmouth, but met his end in 1919 when he was auctioned off for charity as pork. He ultimately raised £1,785 for the Red Cross.[17]

Other pigs have been allowed to live out their lives as pets. Sy Montgomery's *The Good, Good Pig* (2006) tells the story of the pig named Christopher Hogwood, who arrived at Montgomery's rural New Hampshire home as a sick piglet and stayed for fourteen years, weighing close to 340 kg (750 lb) at the time of his

A child putting kitchen waste into a salvage bin for pig food, British Home Front, Second World War.

natural death. Christopher Hogwood became a community icon and was well known throughout New England, thanks to newspaper articles and radio reports about his tremendous fortune in being saved from slaughter by such an indulgent family.[18] Montgomery's bond with Christopher is quite touching, although far from the norm. These stories of exceptional pigs, either kept as pets or somehow rescued from slaughter, ultimately serve as a palliative exception that helps us forget that our dominant relationship with pigs involves killing and eating them.

Perhaps this amnesia about the fate of most pigs explains why people fell in love with Vietnamese potbellied pigs. Beginning in the 1980s, these animals became trendy pets in the USA after being imported into North America by Canadian Keith Connell. In 1986, when the first potbellies were sold in the USA, they cost thousands of dollars. Since then the price has come down substantially. There are also plenty of pigs available for adoption, because many people failed to realize what

A fully grown Vietnamese pot-bellied pig.

A pre-First World War postcard of a pig-drawn carriage.

they were in for when they bought a cute and cuddly piglet. Full-grown Vietnamese potbellied pigs can weigh as much as 91 kg (200 lb) and live for more than a dozen years.[19] So many people abandoned their pet pigs that pig sanctuaries and refuges were established throughout the USA, the earliest founded in 1987, when the first set of imported potbellied pigs became unwanted. Judy Woods, who took in her first potbellied pig in 1992, created one rescue centre, Pigs Peace Sanctuary. She now has almost 200 pigs, mostly potbellies, but with some rescued farm hogs as well, on 34 acres outside of Seattle, Washington. These fortunate pigs will get to live out their lives in comfort, assuming Woods can continue to find funding.[20]

Many owners love their potbellied pigs, of course. One was the actor George Clooney, who reportedly has said that his eighteen-year relationship with his pig Max was the longest relationship he ever had. Interestingly, there are more Vietnamese potbellied pigs in the US than in Vietnam, where the indigenous pig population has declined with the introduction of large breeds of pigs, which are more profitable for local farmers.[21]

Stills from
Operation
Plumbbob,
Nevada Test Site,
1957, in which
1,200 pigs were
exposed to
blast effects
and radiation.

The kinship that some people feel with pigs that makes them partners in work, play and everyday life reflects an awareness of the similarities between humans and pigs. As Sir Winston Churchill reportedly observed, 'I like pigs. Dogs look up to us. Cats look down on us. Pigs treat us as equals.' Similarities between human and pig anatomy and physiology have made pigs important in medical research and human health, although the power in the relationship ultimately resides with the humans.

The anatomy of the pig is sufficiently similar to that of humans that it has been traditional for students to dissect a foetal pig in biology classes to explore the similarities in organ systems, metabolism and basic form. Because of this biological similarity, living pigs were used in many studies of the effects of atomic blasts and radiation during the Cold War. In 1946 Pig 311 was found swimming in the sea after the testing of the atomic bomb at Bikini Atoll. This 'indestructible' pig survived both the sinking of the Japanese cruiser *Sakawa* in the test and a large dose of radiation and was eventually sent to the National Zoo in Washington, DC. As part of 1957's Operation Plumbbob, the biggest and longest series of aboveground nuclear tests held at the Nevada Test Site, military scientists exposed corrals containing 1,200 pigs to atomic fallout and radiation.[22]

In general physicians cannot practise their techniques and procedures on pigs, although the US military has used pigs to train medics serving in Iraq and Afghanistan. Dustin E. Kirby, a Navy trauma medic, was given an anesthetized pig in training, noting, 'The idea is to work with live tissue. You get a pig and you keep it alive. And every time I did something to help him, they would wound him again. So you see what shock does, and what happens when more wounds are received by a wounded creature.' 'My pig? They shot him twice in the face with a 9-millimeter pistol, and then six times with an AK-47 and then twice with a 12-gauge shotgun. And then he was set on fire. I kept him alive for 15 hours. That was my pig.' Animal welfare groups were outraged and reminded the Department of Defense of the sophisticated medical simulators that could be used instead.[23]

Given the use of pigs as stand-ins for human biological processes, it is not surprising that xenotransplantation – the transplantation of living cells, tissues, or organs from one species to another – has been a long-standing goal, albeit one thwarted by technical, legal and moral obstacles. The first use of pig as a source of organs for humans took place in 1906, when a failed attempt was made to implant a pig's liver into a critically ill woman. Although early xenotransplantation research focused on primates, scientists turned to pigs because of the similarity in size between human and pig organs and because of the difficulty of breeding primates in large numbers. The spread of diseases from primates to humans was also a concern. Interestingly, ethical concerns were supposed to be less significant with pigs, as it was assumed that because millions of pigs are killed and eaten, there would be less reluctance to use pigs as sources of organs.[24]

Because the human immune system would recognize pig organs as foreign, scientists quickly understood that pigs would need to be genetically modified. The first transgenic pigs were created in 1995, but there are still technical (as well as legal and ethical) hurdles to overcome. Despite some breakthroughs in genetic modification and cellular manipulation – and the less obviously significant recent breeding of pigs that are tinted green after they were injected with a jellyfish protein as embryos – early optimism about xenotransplantation has largely dissipated, both because funding has been redirected towards human stem cell research and because of concerns about viruses that could potentially pass the species barrier.[25]

While full-scale organ transplantation from pigs to humans still seems quite distant, thousands of people have had heart valve replacement surgery, which can involve either a mechanical valve or a biological one, often from a pig. Porcine valves have been used in open-heart surgery for over twenty years, although they are more frequently implanted into older patients because they only last approximately fifteen years. These valves are chemically treated to kill any pig cells and are implanted with very little risk of rejection.[26]

New medical technologies have outpaced traditional ideas about pigs. Early concerns about whether pig parts or products were appropriate for Jewish patients have been resolved by rabbinical interpretation, even though they recur frequently. Because the Jewish pork taboo does not extend to uses of the pig beyond food, Jewish patients can have heart valves from pigs used in heart valve replacement surgery and can take the blood thinner heparin, which is derived from pigs as well. In a recent discussion of medical ethics and Jewish dietary law, Rabbi Tzvi H. Weinreb of the Orthodox Union noted that 'pig derivatives are only prohibited to be ingested via normal digestive processes. There is no prohibition whatsoever against using or gaining benefit from pig or pig derivatives intravenously or as cosmetics or, for that matter, as the main component of a football.'[27]

Recent genetic modificaions have produced the Enviropig™, which generates manure that is lower in phosphorus, reducing the environmental impacts of large-scale hog farms. In reality, this genetic engineering has produced a 'regulatory-friendly nature' that enables producers to comply with legal restrictions on the waste produced by CAFOs, eliminating a barrier to capitalist accumulation.[28] Another genetic modification of pigs has enabled them to produce heart-healthy omega-3 fatty acids, although government approval is not likely, nor is it clear that consumers would purchase their meat. This news did, however, lead American comedian Jon Stewart to inaugurate a new segment of *The Daily Show* called 'What are we doing to pigs?', in which he commented 'yes, yes, we *could* eat in moderation, but wouldn't it be easier to just rearrange a mammal's cellular structure?'[29]

Some human–pig partnerships are unwanted and detrimental to both species. In 2009 the global media were full of stories about the outbreak of 'swine flu', which the World Health Organization declared a 'public health emergency of international concern'. Swine influenza virus (SIV) is common in pig populations worldwide, although its transmission to humans is rare. If transmission results in human influenza, it is called zoonotic swine flu. During the 1918 flu pandemic, which killed millions worldwide, people realized that pigs were ill at the same time as humans, although it is still unclear whether this strain of influenza went from swine to humans or vice versa. Swine flu outbreaks have occurred occasionally ever since, notably in 1976 in the United States, an episode remembered for the panic that occurred after reports of deaths and neuromuscular disorders that resulted from the vaccinations.[30]

In 1998 pigs throughout the United States became sick from swine flu. Scientists discovered that this virus originated in pigs but with strains of flu from both birds and humans, demonstrating that pigs could serve as crucibles where new flu viruses develop.[31] The 2009 outbreak began in Mexico. Although the culprit was the H1N1 virus, which contains elements of swine, human and avian flu strains, it was immediately labelled the 'swine flu', in part because the first person to be unwell lived near an industrial hog farm. Despite the fact that this influenza is transmitted from person to person (not from pigs to people), cannot be caught from eating pork products and has not been found in American hogs, the name 'swine flu' caught on with the media, angering US pork producers, who faced both a sharp decline of pork sales and the ban on pig and pork exports by more than ten countries.[32] The pork industry is also highly concerned about the possible spread of the H1N1 virus from people to swine, both for its effects on livestock and because widespread transmission from people to pigs could further transform the virus. Pig farmers are vigilant about infectious diseases, which can spread rapidly in confinement-based systems. For example, pseudorabies, a disease caused by a herpes virus which affects pigs' reproductive performance, was first detected in the United States in the nineteenth century, although it only began to cause significant swine losses in the 1960s with the beginning of concentrated production. Today's pigs are sensitive to pathogens, so much so that visitors to modern barns have to don makeshift biohazard suits to protect pigs from germs. Less stringent, though obvious, measures have been taken at agricultural fairs to protect pigs from potentially sick fairgoers.[33]

Because of the emergence of the 'swine flu', the industry has come under renewed attack for its modern pig-farming practices. Commentators referred to the H1N1 pandemic as 'the pigs' revenge' for the pork industry's transformation of hog farming from 'the happy farm depicted in school readers' to 'vast excremental hells, containing tens of thousands of animals with weakened immune systems suffocating in heat and manure while exchanging pathogens at blinding velocity with their fellow inmates'.[34] The American journalist Nicholas Kristof has attacked the use of antibiotics in industrial farming for helping to create 'superbugs' resistant to medication, including a new form of MRSA (methicillin-resistant *Staphylococcus aureus*) that is present in about 25 per cent of American hogs and kills 18,000 Americans annually. He has urged the Obama administration to take action to limit the use of antibiotics, although given the power of agribusiness and the weakness of the Food and Drug Administration, most are sceptical about the prospects for change.[35]

While only time will tell us how significant the current H1N1 pandemic will be for the world's human population, it has already proved both a tragedy and farce for pigs. The only known pig in Afghanistan, an animal named Khanzir ('pig' in Pashto) that was donated to the Kabul Zoo by China, was placed under quarantine because people were worried about getting the flu. The loneliest pig in the world, having already lost his mate to an attack by a bear, thus became somewhat lonelier, separated from the deer and goats he used to socialize with.[36] Meanwhile, following proclamation of the H1N1 pandemic, officials in Egypt ordered the destruction of all 300,000 of the country's pigs, despite the United Nations' mealy-mouthed admonition that this would be 'a real mistake'. The UN and others argued, correctly, that people were not getting infected from pigs but from other people. What was less commented upon was the effect on Egypt's urban ecology and its minority Coptic Christian population. Because of Islamic restrictions on pork, Egyptian pig farmers are Christian and generally poor, subsisting on the collection of garbage, the sale of recyclables and the raising of pigs. They viewed the culling of pigs as yet another attack on their minority community, one that would inevitably lead to a waste disposal crisis. And these fears were correct: four months later the streets of Cairo were filled with rubbish, as those who used to collect rubbish and recyclables while feeding the organic waste to their pigs had stopped doing so. As Moussa Rateb, a former garbage collector and pig owner, put it, 'They killed the pigs, let them clean the city.'[37] These events in Egypt are a reminder of the ways in which pigs are both deeply embedded in human cultures and subject to ambivalence, if not outright hostility. Positive and mutually sustaining relationships between pigs and people are, in the big picture, truly exceptional, given that pigs largely live only to become pork and generally receive more opprobrium than praise.

6 Good Pigs and Bad Pigs

Pigs are exceptional animals: intelligent, social and enthusiastic. While many peoples and cultures, not to mention individual writers, have celebrated the pig, the general response to pigs is utilitarian – they are tasty to eat – and ambivalent, if not negative. The persistent uncertainty about whether pigs are good or bad animals is connected to the lived relationship between humans and pigs. These attitudes reflect a moral ambivalence about the killing of pigs and ideas about pigs themselves, both of which are often factors in conflicts between human social groups.

The novelist and critic John Berger has suggested that the pig suffers from a vestigial primitive dualism toward those animals that were both 'subjected *and* worshipped, bred *and* sacrificed'. He notes that 'The pig is the only animal bred by man entirely for the sake of its meat. It is fed inordinately on garbage in order to make it fat. It becomes dirty because it is kept in a sty. It is made lazy only because it is confined. Yet the pig – not the breeder – is designated piggish.'[1]

The animal, not the humans who use it, here becomes the object of hostility. This is because, as Peter Stallybrass and Allon White have suggested, the pig is 'a site of competing, conflicting and contradictory definitions'. They argue that it was the pig's proximity to humans (sharing space in the farmyard, eating human leftovers, etc.) and the resemblance of pigs, especially

A pig, supposed lover of dirt, turning its nose up at sweet-smelling herbs in an emblem from Joachim Camerarius's collection of animal emblems, *Symbolorum ex re herbaria desumtorum . . .* (1590).

young ones, to humans that accounts for our ambivalence towards them. They note, for example, that pigs provided a useful way for an emergent middle class to distinguish themselves from the masses, arguing that 'to have nothing in common with pigs' was the 'aim of every educated bourgeois subject'.[2] Changes in attitudes towards pigs thus signpost the development of modernity. Pigs increasingly became objects of hatred and abuse, as they were herded into cities and appeared in slums in industrial towns and cities, serving 'as a sign of the gross immiseration of its fellow slum dwellers'.[3]

Pigs were associated with poverty, drunkenness and vice long before they appeared in urban slums, of course. Because drunkenness was seen as the triumph of animal passions over human rationality, Thomas Young's *England's Bane: Or, The Description*

A mummer
from the guild
of butchers with
a pig's head,
costumed for
the Nuremberg
Shrovetide
carnival,
c. 1590–1640.

of Drunkenesse of 1617 described someone as 'sow drunke,' who 'vomits, spewes, and wallowes in the mire, like a Swine'. Edward Schoen's woodcut *Four Properties of Wine* similarly depicted drunkards vomiting and pigs eating it up.[4]

Pigs were also associated with the poor and unruly. One of the earliest negative associations between pigs and the poor comes in John Gower's *Vox Clamantis*, which reflects the terror of propertied men after the Peasants' Rising of 1381. Gower dreamed of a field of marching men who suddenly turned into swine that were 'Not content with acorns for their food, or water for their drink, they devour the rich food in the city and drink good wine, so that they lie in drunkenness, as dead. They despise the pig-sty and defile kings' palaces with their filth', turning the proper order of the world upside-down. Five hundred years later, the poor continued to be referred to as animals because of their association with pigs. In *The Condition of the Working Class in England* of 1844, Friedrich Engels associated the Irish with pigs, writing, 'the Irishman allows the pig to share his own living quarters. This new, abnormal method of rearing livestock in the large towns is entirely of the Irish origin . . . The Irishman lives and sleeps with the pig, the children play with the pig, ride on its back, and roll about in the filth with it.' Engels was wrong about the Irish here, as urban pig-keeping was a common practice, one seen as recently as the 1980s in Vietnam when some Vietnamese raised pigs in their bathrooms to signal their affluence through

'And they say we are pigs', Soviet propaganda poster combating drunkenness, 1958.

urban agriculture. Nevertheless, his work served to naturalize the supposed animality of the Irish, enabling him to depict the English proletariat as improvable. This association of pigs with slum dwellers reached its apex in Henry Mayhew's 1861 *London Labour and the London Poor*, with its vision of 'a race of wild hogs inhabiting the sewers in the neighborhood of Hampstead . . . feeding on the offal and garbage washed into it continually.' These 'ferocious' pigs threaten the elite, who only enjoy pigs when they are on the table.[5]

While attitudes toward pigs worsened in the eighteenth and nineteenth centuries, perhaps there is something deeper in the human–pig relationship that explains the human ambivalence towards pigs. Might disdain for pigs have to do with shame and guilt about our relationship with them? Both physical proximity and physiological similarity encourage identification with pigs, enabling people to recognize qualities in the animal that they

would perhaps prefer not to see in themselves. Perhaps, as one commentator has noted, 'the object of man's peculiar cultural disdain for the pig is less the beast itself than man's own speck-led soul.'[6]

More specifically, perhaps 'the vilification of the pig can be attributed to the need to assuage the guilt of killing and eating such a commensual associate'. This would partly explain the many depictions of pigs in butcher shops and at barbecue stands as willing and happy participants in their own consumption. Might this prevalence of imagery featuring happy pigs asking to be eaten represent an attempt to express respect for the pig amidst the larger denial of what is shared across species lines?[7]

One of the traits attributed to pigs, and by extension to humans, is greed and gluttony. The association of pigs with greed and excess is of long standing. In 1509 Alexander Barclay denounced 'immoderate vyleness' as a characteristic of the pig, adding, 'The swynes lyvynge we all ought to eschewe / In worde and dede we ought to avoyde excesse.' The modern equivalent, perhaps, is the Wall Street saying 'Bulls make money, bears make money, but pigs just get slaughtered!', a judgement which is critical of impatient, emotional and greedy investors.[8]

One often hears references to men as 'pigs' based on their behaviour towards women. The casualness with which that asso-ciation is made reflects a long-standing association between pigs, sex and boorishness. Male pigs have a long, corkscrew-shaped penis (which is where the slang verb 'to screw' comes from) and spend about fifteen minutes mounting the sow, which comes into oestrus every 18–21 days unless pregnant. The sow and the boar may mate several times during oestrus, and if successful, will have a litter of piglets about 115 days later.[9]

The reality of swine intercourse does not, of course, explain the negative association of men and pigs. The term 'male chauvinist

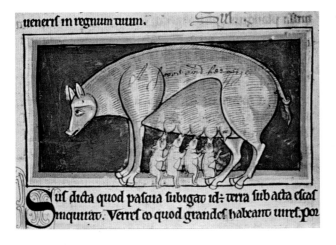

A sow suckling piglets, from a 13th-century bestiary. The sow was identified with sex, fertility, carnality and sin.

pig' became popular in the 1960s, used by feminists to criticize men who freely expressed their belief in the superiority of their gender. This phrase serves to highlight differences between women and men and between humans (male) and animals (female). The writer Ariel Levy titled her 2005 book on women who participate in their own objectification *Female Chauvinist Pigs*. Men were most recently depicted as pigs around women in an international advertising campaign for Trojan condoms. In the ad, anthropomorphized pigs surround women in a bar. When one pig buys a condom from a vending machine in the bathroom, he is suddenly transformed into a good-looking young man. The message to guys: 'Evolve. Use a condom every time.' These ads appeared on television and in print magazines, including women's magazines, where the slogan was modified to 'Evolve: Choose the one who uses a condom every time.'[10]

Women have been objectified and sexualized as animals as well, of course. The cover of *Playboar*, a parody of *Playboy* magazine, is based on the poster for Stanley Kubrick's adaptation of

Female nude with pig, hand-coloured French photograph, c. 1900.

Cover of *The Best of Playboar* (1996).

Nabokov's *Lolita*. Inside, there is a photo of a pig masturbating that references the *Venus of Urbino*. Carol Adams suggests that these pig images make it clear that the purpose of pornography is to reproduce inequality, something made manifest here by replacing women with animals.[11]

To depict or label a person as a swine thus has something to do with power, an association best seen in the vernacular use of 'pig' to deride police officers and others in authority. While we tend to associate this phrasing with the countercultural attitudes of the 1960s, the coupling of the authorities with pigs has a long history. In the 1811 *Lexicon Balatronicum*, a British dictionary of slang and vulgarity, 'pig' was used as an epithet to describe the London police, making the phrase 'floor the pig and bolt' mean 'to knock down the police officer and flee'. In England the term

124

THE BEST OF
PLAYBOAR

TAFFY LOVELY: LITTERMATE OF THE YEAR

SEX SURVEY: 69 QUESTIONS

A SWINE'S GUIDE TO ETIQUETTE

**TELEPHONE SEX:
ARE YOU GETTING IT IN THE EAR?**

THE CURL NEXT DOOR
PHOTO CONTEST

GENUINE PIGSKIN

ONE TIME
COLLECTOR'S
EDITION!

'The Wonderful Miss Atkinson', a pig-faced lady depicted in a print from c. 1815 based on a drawing by George Morland. Legends about wealthy but lonely pig-faced ladies who lived in seclusion were once common, especially in England and Ireland, although public exhibitions usually featured a shaved and dressed black bear.

was 'almost exclusively applied by London thieves to a plain-clothes man, or a "nose"', and was common among the criminal element until it went mainstream in the 1960s. Perhaps the best image of the police as pigs is Ed Belchamber's cover of the 'Special Pig Issue' of *Oz* magazine in May 1971, itself a response to the trial of the 'Oz Three' for obscenity in their 'Schoolkids Issue'. The link between pigs and cops can be hostile, as in graffiti that says 'Fuck the Pigs', or playful, as in the television show *The Simpsons*, in which police chief Clancy Wiggum is depicted as the stereotypical lazy and incompetent cop and as 'a conscious pun' was drawn to resemble a pig.[12]

While this use of pigs to describe others is generally symbolic (although the Yippies did run a live pig named 'Pigasus' for president at the Democratic National Convention in Chicago in 1968), living pigs have often generated conflict. Pigs and other English livestock caused many of the conflicts between the English and Native Americans in early American history. In the nineteenth century a pig nearly inaugurated a shooting war between the

Cover of *Oz* magazine 'Special Pig Issue' (May 1971).

David Fenton,
Yippies Marching
Through the
Streets with
'Pigasus', their
Chosen Candidate
for US President,
New York City,
September 1968.

British and Americans in Oregon. On 15 June 1869 an American squatter asserted his property rights in territory claimed by both nations by shooting a pig rooting in his garden on San Juan Island. Unfortunately, an employee of the Hudson's Bay Company owned the dead pig. When the British authorities threatened to arrest the shooter, Americans on the island called for US military

128

protection. The British, fearing further American occupation of San Juan Island, sent troops and warships, turning the incident into an international crisis. An agreement was reached to jointly occupy the islands, an arrangement that lasted until a final boundary settlement in 1872. The Pig War is commemorated at the San Juan Island National Historic Park and at an annual festival and encampment.[13]

Because of their association with individual and familial self-determination, pigs were often associated with political and moral independence, something recognized by William Cobbett when he wrote in 1821 that 'A couple of flitches of bacon are worth fifty thousand Methodist sermons and religious tracts. The sight

A tapestry from Flanders depicting the countryside in winter, *c.* 1675.

Creole pigs, important economic assets for impoverished families in Haiti.

of them on the rack tends more to keep a man from poaching and stealing than whole volumes of penal statutes, though assisted by the terrors of the hulks and gibbet.' An effort to institutionalize the links between pig-keeping and autonomy was initiated by Civil Rights activist Fannie Lou Hamer, who helped organize the raising of 'freedom hogs' at the Freedom Farms Cooperative (1969–74) in Sunflower County, Mississippi. A 'pig bank' gave sows to needy families. Once the sow had a litter, the family was to give two pigs back to the bank. This local development programme, she recalled, 'helped us toward real freedom' and perhaps served as a model for today's Heifer Project International programmes.[14]

Autonomy can be taken away as well as given, as was evidenced by the fate of the *kochon kreyol* in Haiti. In the late 1970s African swine fever was detected in pigs in the Dominican Republic and Haiti. Fearing the spread of the disease into its pork industry, the US government backed a multinational campaign to eradicate all the pigs in both countries. In Haiti nearly 1.3 million pigs were destroyed under the Programme pour l'Eradication de la

Peste Porcine Africaine et pour le Développement de l'Elvage Porcin (PEPPADEP), with devastating effects on the population. Haitian pigs – *kochon kreyol* – were hearty but scrawny black pigs that were adapted to local conditions. More importantly, they literally served as 'piggy banks', providing rural Haitians with a living savings account that could be sold or slaughtered to pay for religious ceremonies, health care and schooling. Within months of the completion of pig eradication in August 1984, school attendance dropped, malnutrition increased and religious life – both Catholic and vodoun – was disrupted. In the long term, this neo-imperialist pig eradication accelerated the movement of rural Haitians into cities and contributed to the deforestation crisis, as people cut down trees to make charcoal that they could sell to augment their incomes.

To make matters worse, the pigs sent to replace the *kochon kreyol* were much more fragile and only thrived on expensive enriched feed. Costs of preparing for and feeding one of the replacement pigs (often called *prince à quatre pieds*, 'four-footed princes') exceeded most Haitians' annual income. To even receive one of these American *kochon blan* one had to agree to construct a tin-roofed and concrete-floored shelter for the animal, a dwelling that was in many cases nicer than most Haitians' own homes. In short, the PEPPADEP operation was a disaster, one seen in racial and class terms by Haitians themselves, who identified with the black but hearty pigs doomed for the sake of fat, white, spoiled pigs from the north. Now understood as a classic example of how foreign aid can undermine the aided, one Haitian best summed up his feelings about this American project by commenting: 'Now they come back and make money selling us their hotdogs!'[15]

Although living pigs have caused trouble throughout the world, pigs are also mobilized symbolically in political and cultural disputes. The manipulation of ideas about pigs in human

ah! Le Maudit animal, il m'a tant géné pour s'engrauser, il est si gras,
qu'il en en est Ladre. je reviens du marché, je ne sais plus qu'en faire.

Louis XVI
represented
as a human-pig
hybrid, in a French
Revolutionary
print.

politics was perhaps most pervasive in the late eighteenth century, when words and pictures relating to pigs reflected tensions surrounding the implications of the American and French Revolutions. Pigs were typically reviled in satires and caricatures, most famously when Edmund Burke used his description of the 'swinish multitude' in his *Reflections on the Revolution in France* (1790) to describe the threat posed by democracy and the corresponding need for hierarchy, order and deference. The 'learned pig', which seemed to invert categories of high and low, appeared in many American satires and was often used to critique citizens of the new nation who were thought to have reached beyond their proper station. In response, many embraced identification with pigs and the public so derided by elites, including Robert

132

Southey, who signed his letters with the initials 'O.S.M.' to proudly declare that he was 'one of the swinish multitude'.[16]

The use of pigs in political discourse was not confined to debates about the nature of the public in the eighteenth century. In fact, porcine imagery was ubiquitous in the 2008 presidential election in the United States. While much of the talk was about 'earmarks' (itself a term related to agriculture in that an 'earmark' is made to show ownership of cattle, pigs and sheep), what was really at issue was traditional 'pork barrel' politics. The modern sense of the term – spending used to benefit constituents of a given politician in return for votes or campaign contributions – dates to the late nineteenth century, when references to 'pork' were common in discussions of Congress; an 1873 Ohio newspaper denounced the 'many previous visits to the public pork-barrel'. Today, a Washington watchdog group publishes an annual 'Congressional Pig Book' that lists projects it considers to be wasteful expenditures that serve only a local or special interest.[17]

A minor squabble ensued when Democratic presidential candidate Barack Obama used a pig-related idiom in telling a crowd of supporters, 'You can put lipstick on a pig, but it's still a pig.' Republicans saw this as an attack on their vice-presidential candidate, Sarah Palin, a self-described 'pit bull with lipstick'. Obama's comment was actually intended as an indictment of Republican candidate John McCain's policies. While many commentators thought the phrase was quite old, in this formulation it only dates back to 1985, although Charles F. Lummis, editor of the *Los Angeles Times*, wrote in 1926 that 'Most of us know as much of history as a pig does of lipsticks.' There is a long history of porcine proverbs that describe efforts to convert the useless to the useful, the ugly to pretty. The maxim 'You can't make a silk purse from a sow's ear' dates back to the mid-sixteenth century. In 1732 British doctor Thomas Fuller commented, 'A hog in

us Civil War-era envelope satirizing the Confederate General P.G.T. Beauregard. When turned length-wise the image presents a caricature of the general in a jester's hat.

armour is still but a hog', a phrase adapted by the 1880s to 'A hog in a silk waistcoat is still a hog.' Ultimately, these formulations assert, one's nature cannot be changed, even by improved circumstances.[18]

In preparations for the 2007–8 Year of the Pig in China, images of pigs were banned from appearing on state-run Chinese television 'to avoid conflicts with ethnic minorities'. While only 2 per cent of China's population is Muslim, the goal was to create a harmonious relation between the dominant Han Chinese and ethnic minorities. Historians have noted that Han are generally sensitive about Muslim attitudes towards pigs, although there have been some tensions where Han and the historically Muslim Hui live in close proximity. While some conservative Hui won't mention the word for 'pig' (often using euphemisms like 'black bug' or 'black bastard'), lineage and ancestry, rather than cultural traditions, are most central to the identity of Chinese Muslims, reducing the chance that pigs will provoke conflict.[19]

Unsurprisingly, the taboos against pigs in Judaism and Islam have been mobilized symbolically and practically in the wake of the terrorist attacks in the United States, Spain and Britain.

Greater attention has been paid to the relationship between Muslims and pigs, sometimes in the interest of accommodation and friendship, but also in efforts to create greater hostilities in what some view as a clash of civilizations. In the UK a so-called controversy developed when libraries removed books about pigs from their shelves and a school in Huddersfield changed the title of a student production of Roald Dahl's 'The Three Little Pigs' (from *Revolting Rhymes*, 1982) to 'The Three Little Puppies' to avoid making Muslim children feel uncomfortable singing about pigs. Many saw this as political correctness gone mad, especially since there were no complaints from the Muslim community about these books or performances. There is no prohibition in Islam against mentioning pigs, making one wonder if the very circulation of these stories is largely designed to support popular conservatism, which is generally hostile toward Islam.[20]

In contrast to the apparent sensitivity of the British, Norwegians and Americans have proven much more aggressive in

'The Christian Pig is Put to Death' – executing pig-like or sheep-like Christians in an 1890s Chinese woodcut.

their use of pigs in the war against 'islamofacism'. In Norway anti-immigrant politicians threatened to use 'porcine tactics' to chase Muslims from the public square in Bergen if they used it for prayer while awaiting completion of their mosque, suggesting that 'residents should hang up pig's feet and play pig squeals over loudspeakers to scare off Muslims'. In a disturbing throwback to (unconfirmed) stories about how the United States military attempted to put down the Moro Rebellion (1899–1913) against American occupation of the Philippines by killing Muslim Filipino revolutionaries and burying their bodies with pigs, one Norwegian politician claimed to have used these 'porcine tactics' when he was a soldier for the United Nations in Somalia and Lebanon in the 1990s. In Katy, Texas, Craig Barker was angry at an Islamic association's plans to build a mosque next to his property, so he held weekly pig races and sold sausages in protest. Other than generating media coverage, however, the overall effect was minimal.[21]

Real trouble has occurred in Israel, where in the 1990s some Soviet-born Jews enlisted the pig into their war against Arabs. In the summer of 1997 Tatiana Susskin distributed posters of Mohammed with a pig's head throughout Hebron, provoking riots and calls for vengeance. She spent sixteen months in jail after being convicted in an Israeli court of a racist and religious offence. Avigdor Eskin was indicted for placing a pig's head on the grave of Izz ad-Din al-Quassam, the Palestinian preacher and militia leader who was killed by the British in 1935. Eskin was stopped, thankfully, before he could catapult a pig's head with a Qu'ran in its mouth onto the Temple Mount.[22]

These divisions between religious and national groups, marked by contrasting attitudes about both real and symbolic pigs, highlight the hold pigs have on the human imagination. Whether seen positively or negatively, pigs are good to think with, providing people with ways to understand and talk about their world. Accordingly, pigs have shaped human language and culture, including literature and art that, at its best, urges us to think about the lives of pigs.

7 Pigs of the Imagination

Pigs are aware beings with minds of their own that have long posed a dilemma for humans torn between seeing 'pigs' and 'pork'. An extensive literature, art and popular culture has imagined human kinship with pigs, often interrogating the tension between the pig's similarity to humans and its usual fate as meat. Some of this material deals with actual pigs and their biological presence or absence. In other cases, pigs have shaped our language and culture and captured the imagination as tropes and metaphors. Pigs have also been the subject of children's literature and staples in cartoons, television and film, often taking anthropomorphic form. Musical, visual and material representations of pigs also explore the closeness and distance humans keep with pigs.

The long relationship between humans and pigs has shaped the English language and Western culture. Pigs have given their name to a number of non-animal related items, including porcelain (named for its similarity in appearance to a cowrie shell, itself named for its resemblance to *porcellana*, literally little pig, but also meaning vulva in Italian), pig iron (because the mould created smaller ingots – the pigs – attached to a central runner – the sow), and the scraper pig, a device used to clear buildup from pipeline walls.[1]

While these terms all have something to do with the resemblance of an item to pigs, some pig-related phrases, like 'piggyback'

and, originally, 'piggy bank', have nothing to do with actual pigs. In the case of the coin accumulator, the Middle English word 'pygg' referred to a type of clay used to make jars. People saved money in 'pygg jars', which over time became known as 'pygg banks'. Eventually potters crafted these containers to resemble their name and by the eighteenth century a pig-shaped 'piggy bank' was fairly common. There is an important relationship between the 'piggy bank' and the pig itself, for just as farmers would feed scraps and leftovers to their pig to fatten it up for eventual slaughter, children would fill their piggy bank with coins only to break it open when full. Hans Christian Andersen's 'The Money-Pig' of 1855 describes a clay piggy bank that was 'stuffed so full that it could no longer rattle, which is the highest state of perfection to which a money-pig can attain'. Early pig-shaped piggy banks are quite collectible, as many of them were destroyed in the process of being emptied. Today, they are likely to be made with a plug in the bottom so one does not have to destroy the piggy bank to get at its contents.[2]

In contrast to using a piggy bank to save money, to 'pig out' is to do something with gluttonous abandon, to overindulge. To be 'pigheaded' means one is being stubborn. We say that we 'sweat like pigs' – that is, a lot – even though pigs do not sweat at all. And even though pigs are actually quite clean animals if left to their own devices, separating their sleeping area from where they defecate, for example, we refer to a dirty or messy room as a 'pig-sty'. It is this connotation that led undergraduates at Oxford to say that to 'keep a pig' was to have to share a room with a fellow student. 'Hogwash' means empty or pretentious talk and is a term taken from the garbage or slop fed to pigs. 'Hog wild' means wildly excited, although to 'pig it' is to stop running when one is tired.[3]

'Pig Tail' was a term used to refer to the Chinese, based on the way they wore their hair in a queue. 'Pig' was also applied to a person who was sloppy in appearance, loose in morals or both. A 'Pig Islander' was a New Zealander, and a 'long pig' is a person who might be meat for cannibals, reflecting rumours that human flesh and pork taste similar. A 'pigskin' is a reference to an American football, even though those footballs are made from cowhide. A 'blind pig' was an unlicensed or illegal saloon or speakeasy, where one might drink 'pig sweat' – beer or cheap whisky – and eat a 'pig between two sheets' – a ham sandwich. In hobo slang, a 'hog' always referred to a locomotive, but for motorcycle buffs, it can only refer to a Harley-Davidson. We also use the phrases 'happy as a pig in shit' and 'happy as a pig in

clover' (the latter is apparently more American) to convey pleasure and contentment. 'Hog heaven', of course, is paradise.[4]

Pigs are associated with luck as well as happiness. This belief developed in Germany and, while prevalent in the late nineteenth and early twentieth centuries, persists today. In Germany one brings marzipan pigs to people for good luck at Christmas, the New Year and on their birthday. A roast pork dinner on Christmas Eve was also believed to promote good luck. One can find hundreds of vintage postcards with different designs featuring lucky pigs. Many feature pigs with other good luck charms, such as the four-leaf clover, and with symbols of prosperity, including money. The tradition of breaking a peppermint pig with a hammer and sharing the pieces to ensure health, happiness and prosperity after a holiday meal was invented in Saratoga, New York, in the 1880s. It is one of few holiday traditions indigenous to America. The marzipan and peppermint pig traditions have been turned into children's books and videos and given the name to a record by the Cocteau Twins.[5]

The phrase 'living high off the hog' refers to the most tender and expensive cuts of meat, just as to 'scrape the bottom of the barrel' means to be in a desperate situation, referring to the way a family could go hungry once they could see the bottom of their barrel of pork. To be 'as independent as a hog on ice' has been thought to refer to both the awkward and insecure way a live pig would be on a frozen surface and to the indifference of a slaughtered pig packed on ice for preservation. Pigs, of course, would prefer the former.[6]

'Root, hog, or die' is an old American idiom for self-reliance, reflecting the way pigs were turned out to seek sustenance on their own. It makes an early printed appearance in the autobiography of Davy Crockett, the famous frontiersman, where he refers to it as an 'old saying'. In the nineteenth century many American songs took 'Root, Hog, or Die' as their title and theme, referring to American independence, frontier settlers' autonomy and the experiences of the California Gold Rush and military service in the Civil War.[7] Woody Guthrie mobilized the phrase in a song lamenting the execution of Sacco and Vanzetti, while Mojo Nixon and Skid Roper used it as the title of their 1989 rockabilly record.

The phrase 'when pigs fly', meaning that something is not going to happen, comes from an old Scottish proverb. Lewis Carroll's *Alice's Adventures in Wonderland* of 1865 made the concept famous when the Duchess responds to Alice's claim that she has a right to think by commenting, 'Just about as much right as pigs have to fly'. The idea of being grounded yet aspiring to

'If it had grown up it would have made a dreadfully ugly child: but it makes rather a handsome pig, I think': Alice and the Pig Baby – John Tenniel's illustration for Lewis Carroll's *Alice's Adventures in Wonderland* (1865).

better things led John Steinbeck to use Pigasus, the flying pig, as his personal symbol. The flying pig has become the symbol of the American city of Cincinnati, giving its name to a marathon and to a local ale. Statues of flying pigs can be found throughout 'Porkopolis'. Given the long use of the idiom, the aviator Lord Brabazon carried a small piglet in a basket on board a 1909 flight. The sign on the pig's basket read: 'I am the first pig to fly'.[8]

Pigs have a long history in Western literature for adults and children. Young children and their parents share the nursery rhyme 'This Little Piggy Went to Market', medieval schoolboys

laughed at the parody *Testamentum Porcelli* ('The Testament of
the Piglet'), young adults read of the downfall of the boy nicknamed 'Piggy' in William Golding's *Lord of the Flies*, and adults
have followed the history of the Empress of Blandings, the Berkshire sow at the centre of many of P. G. Wodehouse's novels.
While pigs appear in a wide range of literary forms for different
ages, pigs seem especially significant in children's fiction, where
they play different roles and impart different lessons.

In the nineteenth century pigs in children's literature were
often used to remind young readers not to stray beyond their
proper station. The *Little Pig's Ramble from Home* urges youth not

Wounded, weary, and hungry, poor Jack now felt sad,
And thought of the home, so safe, he once had.
Where he'd plenty of food, and clean straw for his bed,
And at night, a roof of good thatch o'er his head.
He escaped from the field, though he hardly knew how,
And scampered as fast as his strength would allow;
In the distance, a town, long and wide he could see:—
"Ah! ah!" said Jack swine, "that's the quarter for me."

So Jack hurried on to the city so gay,
Where he walked through the streets in comic array,
But think of his horror, oh! think of his dread,
When, hanging immediately over his head,
In the first butcher's shop that he chanced to discover,
Were the mortal remains of poor Bobby, his brother.
"'Tis sad, sighed our Jack, such a difference should be
Between that unfortunate fellow and me."

to put on airs by following Jack Pig, who dons a wig and top hat and walks upright like a human, but receives his comeuppance when he discovers how pigs are 'dressed' at the butcher's shop. In Thomas Hood's *The Headlong Career and Woful* [*sic*] *Ending of Precocious Piggy*, the titular swine leaves the farm to seek his fortune. After trying out a number of careers and adopting the latest and most fashionable clothes, he attends a country fair, takes to drink and ultimately meets his end at the butcher shop.[9]

Starting in the later nineteenth century images of pigs became a little more playful, although the spectre of the character becoming bacon remained. Beatrix Potter's *The Tale of Little Pig Robinson* (1930) tells the story of how the pig in Edward Lear's poem 'The Owl and the Pussycat' got to 'the land where the Bong-tree grows'. The little pig, sent on errands by his aunts, is abducted by a sailor and impressed into a ship's gang to be fattened up. The ship's cat notifies Little Pig about the cook's intention, and together they plan the pig's escape to the land of the Bong-tree. The aunts, meanwhile, 'led prosperous uneventful lives, and their end was bacon', unlike, presumably, the protagonist. Potter's *The Tale of Pigling Bland* of 1913 is a love story, one that emerged from her life at Hill Top Farm in the Lake District, known for its excellent pigs, and Potter's own ambivalence about pigs, one of which she kept as a kind of pet.[10]

Piglet, one of the most famous fictional pigs in children's literature, made his debut in A. A. Milne's *Winnie-the-Pooh* in 1926. This 'Very Small Animal', illustrated by E. H. Shepard, lived in a house in a large beech-tree. Piglet is easily frightened, but nevertheless tries to be courageous, even when trapped during a flood. As he notes, 'It's a little Anxious to be a Very Small Animal Entirely Surrounded by Water'. Although Piglet did not appear in Walt Disney's 1966 adaptation of *Winnie-the-Pooh*, protests by fans of Milne's books led to Piglet's reintroduction in 1968's

PIGGY GOES FOR A WIG.

'Piggy Goes for a Wig', from Thomas Hood's *The Headlong Career and Woful Ending of Precocious Piggy* (1859).

Winnie the Pooh and the Blustery Day. Piglet stars in his own films now, including *Piglet's Big Movie* (2003), and is a staple of Disney merchandising, having come a long way from the original toys that belonged to the real Christopher Robin Milne.[11]

The first printed version of the story of the *Three Little Pigs* was included in James Orchard Halliwell-Phillipps's *Nursery Rhymes and Nursery Tales* in 1843, although the tale itself is presumably much older. The story should be quite familiar: three little pigs are pursuing their fortune in a dangerous world. The first pig builds a house of straw, but the wolf blows it down and

P. Pig.

eats the pig. The second pig builds a house of sticks, with the same result. The third pig, however, builds a house of bricks that the wolf cannot 'huff and puff' enough to blow down. The wolf tries to sneak down the chimney, but plunges into a pot of boiling water that the pig has prepared for him, outsmarted into becoming the pig's dinner.

There have been countless variations of the Three Little Pigs story over the years. Over time, the violence of the original has been sanitized, and most modern versions allow the first two pigs to escape to join the third, rather than being killed and eaten. There are two subgenres of the story: postmodern revisions of the story include Jon Scieszka's *The True Story of the Three Little Pigs* (which tells the story from the wolf's perspective, who claims to have been framed) and David Weisner's Caldecott-award-winning *The Three Pigs* (in which the pigs are blown from the pages of the book). Regional variations include titles like *Three Little Cajun Pigs*, the bilingual *Los Tres Cerditos*, and *The Three Little Javelinas*.

The most popular anthropomorphic pig character in contemporary children's literature is Olivia, the stubborn yet charming piglet with a passion for opera and ballet created by Ian Falconer. When asked why he chose a pig for his character, Falconer responded, 'pigs are shaped like little kids. Their bodies are smaller than their heads. Pigs are supposed to be intelligent, smarter than dogs, but they're a bit awkward. Their trotters are like little kids' arms that don't work very well yet.'[12] Falconer's minimalist style and stories of a hyperactive piglet who tests her mother's patience found a wide audience, so much so that the US Postal Service included Olivia as one of eight characters in their 'Favorite Children's Book Animals' stamp series. Of the eight animals, two were pigs: Olivia and another 'terrific' pig named Wilbur.

Although *Charlotte's Web*, written in 1952, constantly appears on lists of the greatest children's books ever written, the best thing that E. B. White wrote about pigs was his moving 1948 essay 'Death of a Pig'. In it, White describes the 'antique pattern' of buying a pig in spring, feeding it and killing it in winter as 'a tragedy enacted on most farms with perfect fidelity to the original script'. The completion of this seasonal ritual is thwarted, however, when his pig becomes sick. White describes the days and nights spent taking care of the sick pig, linking the pig's flagging health to his sense of his own physical deterioration, realizing that 'what could be true of my pig could be true also of the rest of my tidy world'. When his pig eventually dies it receives a simple burial. White concludes: 'The loss we felt was not the loss of ham but the loss of pig. He had evidently become precious to me, not that he represented a distant nourishment in a hungry time, but that he had suffered in a suffering world.'[13]

Critics have argued that White wrote *Charlotte's Web* to save this pig in retrospect, as it were. In this story, eight-year-old Fern Arable protests her father's planned elimination of a runt piglet. Demanding 'justice', she adopts the piglet, names him Wilbur and daydreams about him in class, as older girl would dream about a boy. Wilbur lives with Fern for a few weeks and then is sold to her uncle, Homer Zuckerman. Although Fern visits as often as she can, Wilbur gets lonely and bored; after all, he basically does what real pigs do: eat, sleep and stand around. Looking for a friend, he finds Charlotte, a grey spider. Shortly thereafter, the sheep notify Wilbur that he is being fattened up to be killed: 'Almost all young pigs get murdered by the farmer as soon as the real cold weather sets in.' Knowing that this is true, yet not wanting Wilbur to hear this news, 'Fern grew rigid on her stool', unable to protest as she did at the start of the book. Instead, Charlotte becomes the fighter against injustice, referring to the plan to kill Wilbur as 'the dirtiest trick I ever heard of'.

Charlotte spins a web with the words 'SOME PIG' in it. Oddly, the humans think that this 'miracle' indicates that 'It's the pig that's unusual', not the literate arachnid. Wilbur's reputation grows as Charlotte weaves other legends: 'TERRIFIC', and, later,

Wilbur the pig and Charlotte the spider, in a film adaptation of *Charlotte's Web* (dir. Winick, 2006).

'RADIANT'. Wilbur becomes 'Zuckerman's famous pig', sent to the summer-ending County Fair for show, with Charlotte travelling in Wilbur's crate in case she is needed. At the fair Wilbur receives a special ribbon, guaranteeing his existence through the winter, while Fern finally starts running around with boys. Before the fair closes, Charlotte weaves her last message, 'HUMBLE', over Wilbur's pen. Before dying, Charlotte creates her egg sac, which the rat Templeton helps move to the crate and back to the farm. The book ends with Wilbur revelling in the hatching of Charlotte's children in the spring.[14]

Charlotte's Web lyrically describes farm animals and their environment, providing what White called a 'hymn to the barn'. Fern links the human and animal worlds as the only human who can hear the animals' conversations. Her mother worries about all the time she spends in the barn, but the doctor assures her that 'spiders and pigs were fully as interesting' as boys and besides, everything changes. The implication is that adults are not as attentive to nature and animals, and that in their innocence, children can hear animals' voices and better understand their circumscribed lives. *Charlotte's Web* reflects the human desire to get into the minds of animals. White gives Wilbur enough consciousness to think about the past and the future and, most importantly, to love life and fear death. His simplicity and groundedness, in short, his pig-ness, helps to account for the way this fictional character has shaped the way many people think about living pigs.[15]

Charlotte's Web works because the animals are not asked to do too much. In contrast, Freddy, the star of 26 popular books written by Walter R. Brooks and illustrated by Kurt Weise between 1927 and 1958, is given many things to do. Although he sleeps, daydreams and eats too much, he is motivated into action by an innate sense of justice, assuming guises as a detective, pilot, cowboy, politician and more to solve problems on Bean Farm and elsewhere. Although the series fell out of print, a group called Friends of Freddy helped keep the flame alive and the books are again available. With a film adaptation in the works, Freddy, the 'smallest and cleverest' of the pigs on the Bean Farm, can be expected to do interesting things, because 'when a lazy person once really gets started doing things, it's easier to keep on than it is to stop'.[16]

Another pig with a 'can do!' attitude is the star of Dick King-Smith's novella *The Sheep-Pig* of 1983. King-Smith raised pigs at his Woodlands Farm, near Bristol, England. He got the idea for *The Sheep-Pig* while tending the Guess-the-Weight-of-the-Pig stall at the village fair. As he recalls it, 'I must, I suppose, have thought as I stood upon the village green, recording people's guesses and taking their money, that it was a shame that such a lovely little pink pig should end up, once he was big enough, in the deep freeze. Suppose fate had something quite different in store for him? Suppose he should go and live on a farm, with a sheepdog as his foster mother? Suppose he should want to do what she did? He couldn't be a sheepdog. But he could be a sheep-pig.'[17]

In the book, Mr Hoggett, a sheep farmer, wins a piglet at the county fair, delighting his wife, who hopes to fatten up the 'little porker' for Christmas dinner. The scared little pig is be-friended by one of the farm's sheepdogs, who introduces Babe to the hierarchy of the farm animals. Eventually, Babe saves the sheep from rustlers, earning the trust of Farmer Hoggett, who lets the pig accompany him to the sheep's pastures. One day Hoggett asks the pig to round up the sheep. To the human's surprise, Babe successfully does this, although only after he stops trying to act like the sheepdogs, who use the threat of vio-lence to move the sheep. Instead, Babe models another path to hegemony, asking the sheep politely to line up appropriately. Ultimately, Hoggett enters Babe in the county sheepdog trials, where the pig runs into unfamiliar sheep that will not respond to his requests until he gives them the proper password. The pig performs perfectly, without any commands from Hoggett, stunning the crowd, which breaks out in rapturous applause when the final gate is shut. The story ends with Hoggett looking down at his sheep-pig, telling him, 'That'll do.'

Unlike *Charlotte's Web*, where a talented spider saves Wilbur, here Babe escapes his inevitable death through his own talents in cross-species communication. While in E. B. White's book Fern serves as translator between human and animal worlds, Dick King-Smith has no human who is able to hear the animals' conversations, although Hoggett does understand his animals. In fact, Hoggett and Babe are depicted as having an ideal relationship, one in which the human transcends his culture's expectations of pigs, enabling him to see the potential in an animal otherwise destined for the dinner table.[18]

Chris Noonan's 1995 film adaptation, retitled *Babe*, remains true to the book, but with one crucial distinction: it begins with a recognition of factory farming. We see a sow nursing her piglets, but a voice-over tells us that they live 'in a cruel and sunless world'. The sow is taken away by workers and replaced with a metal udder as a piglet looks through the bars of the confinement system and says, 'Goodbye Mom'. The film thus begins with a glimpse of the horrors faced by actual pigs, making the story of this particular pig even sweeter. Audiences are moved, often to tears, at the end of the film, when Babe successfully pens the sheep. But perhaps this happy ending, as with other tales of exceptional pigs that manage to escape their fate, only serves to enable us to continue to excuse the mainstream killing of pigs.

Babe was a critical and popular success, in part because its mix of living and animatronic animals created such believable characters. The film as a whole ultimately works against the interests of the meat industrial complex by showing animals with their own fully developed lives and communities that do not want to be eaten. Indeed, the film seems to have led some consumers to forsake pork at the request of their children, as it was reported to have led to a 40 per cent drop in pork consumption in Australia. In the United States, where the pork industry was promoting their product as 'the other white meat', it certainly was not helpful to have children and adults rooting for an adorable sheep-herding piglet.[19]

Anthropomorphized animals star in George Orwell's *Animal Farm* (1945), which addressed the Russian Revolution and its aftermath in the form of a barnyard fable. Inspired by animated cartoons, literary works like *Gulliver's Travels* and Orwell's own experiences in Spain, *Animal Farm* begins with a speech by old Major, a prize-winning boar who shares his dream of a world where animals will be free of human oppression and live in equality and peace. Clever pigs, the 'brainworkers' of Manor Farm, lead this revolution, which produces an exhilarating new world of equality and friendship:

> The animals were happy as they had never conceived it possible to be. Every mouthful of food was an acute positive pleasure, now that it was truly their own food, produced by themselves and for themselves, not doled out to them by a grudging master . . . Everyone worked according to his capacity . . . Nobody stole, nobody grumbled over his rations, the quarreling and biting and jealousy which had been normal features of life in the old days had almost disappeared.[20]

A pig bringing prosperity in an early 20th-century French postcard.

Orwell shared this dream of egalitarian socialism and in his essays and letters was critical of the way 'unconsciously power-hungry people' had distorted the socialist movement. He described the turning point of his story as when the pigs Napoleon and Snowball, representing Stalin and Trotsky, first take the milk and apples for themselves. Their propagandist, Squealer, justifies their takings, but as the book progresses, greater amounts of force and intimidation are used to sustain the pigs' dominance. Finally, in Orwell's famous phrase, the farm becomes a place where 'All animals are equal but some animals are more equal than others.' By the end of the book, the pigs have moved into the farmhouse and started acting human: walking on their hind legs, wearing clothes and drinking up the profits from the rendering of the hard-working and loyal horse Boxer. The animals left living outdoors on the farm 'looked from pig to man, and from man to pig, and from pig to man again; but already it was impossible to say which was which'. From the perspective of the dominated, there has only been a changing of the guard.[21]

Animal Farm was a huge success in Britain, although it became even more iconic in the USA, where it caught the popular imagination amid Cold War anxieties. Orwell was upset with the misreading of *Animal Farm* as an anti-Communist polemic, complaining to Dwight Macdonald in 1946, 'If people think I'm defending the status quo, that is, I think, because they have grown pessimistic and assume that there is no alternative except dictatorship or laissez-faire capitalism . . . What I was trying to say was, "You can't have a revolution unless you make it for yourself; there is no such thing as a benevolent dictatorship."'[22]

In the 1950s Orwell's totalitarian pigs became a Cold War trope, thanks to the novel and the 1954 animated feature-length film adaptation. Made in Britain with funding from the American Central Intelligence Agency (CIA), this *Animal Farm* featured a feel-good anti-Communist epilogue where the animals revolt against the pigs, highlighting both the power and the limitations of Orwell's animal allegory, which could be variously interpreted and mobilized to multiple political positions.[23] While the book became a curricular staple and a Cold War master-text, the 1999 film version featuring *Babe*-style animatronic animals was poorly received, perhaps lacking the proper Cold War context. Orwell's work remains memorable, however, for its vision of deceitful, manipulative, greedy and exploitative pigs. In *Animal Farm*, Mr Pilkington, the capitalist who sees the farm as a model for class exploitation, concludes: 'Between pigs and human beings there was not and there need not be any clash of interests whatsoever.' Of course, outside of the realm of fiction, those interests are inevitably incommensurate.[24]

Pigs have been the subject of much poetry and music, from Robert Southey's defence of the pig against its detractors ('The Pig', 1799) to Roald Dahl's tale of the 'wonderfully clever pig' who realized he only existed to be eaten and decides to eat the farmer first ('The Pig', 1970). Sylvia Plath and Ted Hughes commemorated the same animal in, respectively, 'Sow' and 'View of a Pig'. Plath's poem described a neighbour's great sow as 'A monument prodigious in gluttonies', while Hughes wrote of the same pig that, now slaughtered, 'lay on a barrow dead' whose 'weight oppressed me' and was 'too dead now to pity . . . Too deadly factual'.[25]

Significant for its imaginative identification with the animal is Denise Levertov's cycle of poems *Pig Dreams: Scenes From the Life of Sylvia* (1981), which traces the pig's spiritual development from birth to enlightenment and argues for the mutual interdependence of all things. The pig Sylvia condemns the way humans restrict animals' lives, observing

> . . . us they fatten,
> us they exchange for this [money];
> and they breed us not that our life
> may be whole, pig-life
> thriving alongside dog-life, bird-life,
> grass-life, all
> the lives of earth-creatures,
> but that we may be devoured.[26]

In Philip Levine's 'Animals Are Passing From Our Lives', a pig on the way to market imagines his impending death yet retains his dignity, digging in his heels and refusing to be objectified. The pig concludes:

> . . . The boy
> who drives me along believes
>
> that any moment I'll fall
> on my side and drum my toes

like a typewriter or squeal
and shit like a new housewife

discovering television,
or that I'll turn like a beast
cleverly to hook his teeth
with my teeth. No. Not this pig.[27]

Sadly, fewer musicians than poets have attempted to identify imaginatively with the lives and deaths of pigs. Pigs are, however, useful in musical discourse, in part because poor performances can be associated with the squealing and grunting of pigs. Louis XI had a pig orchestra 'conducted' by means of a gallery where the pigs were pierced by spikes to make them squeal. These cruelly treated 'musical pigs' may have been the inspiration for the 1867 American satirical song and print 'La Piganino', which critiqued both amateur musicians and the contemporary vogue for all things Italian.[28]

Every culture entangled with pigs has a way to represent the sounds that pigs make, of course, with 'oink, oink' preferred in English. Humans imitate pigs more precisely on the farm and have developed a series of musical pig calls to bring home the bacon. In 'Pig-Hoo-o-o-o-ey!', P. G. Wodehouse compiled many American regional variations, which included the 'Poig, Poig, Poig' of Wisconsin, 'Kus, Kus, Kus' of Iowa, and 'Loo-ey, Loo-ey, Loo-ey' of Ohio.[29] Hog calling contests, often combined with husband calling contests, remain regular staples at agricultural fairs.

Pigs appear in a wide range of popular music, from Vic Damone's 1950 hit 'Cincinnati Dancing Pig', which refers to the skills of a 'barnyard mister big', to songs of a more metaphorical bent, like Black Sabbath's 'War Pigs', Pink Floyd's 'Pigs on

La Piganino, an anonymous 1860s American lithograph illustration for a popular song satirizing amateur musicians and the vogue for all things Italian.

the Wing' and The Beatles' 'Piggies', in which 'the bigger piggies in the starched white shirts . . . need a damn good whacking'. The British band Pink Floyd was especially enamoured of the flying pig and went to great expense to create a large inflatable pig to fly over Battersea Power Station for the cover of the album *Animals*. During the photo shoot in December 1976, the 12-metre (40-foot) inflatable pig broke loose in strong winds and travelled through the flight path of planes that were landing at Heathrow Airport before finally landing on a farm in Kent.[30] The finest musical invocation of pigs occurs in Robert Wyatt's 'Pigs . . . (In There)', originally commissioned for Victor Schonfeld's 1982 *The Animals Film*. Over a catchy synthesizer and drum track, Wyatt ponders what the confinement operation he sees on a pleasant country drive in Wiltshire 'must be like from the inside'. His questioning refrain, 'Pigs? In There?', highlights the disjunction between our expectations and the reality of how pigs live.

Because pigs are fun to draw and funny to look at, they feature in illustrated form outside of children's picture books. In

Al Capp's classic comic strip *Li'l Abner* the Yokums' pet pig was named Salomey, a pun on both salami and Salome. She was kidnapped in a 1942 story by J. R. Fangsley, 'the world's greatest sportsman hogbreeder', who hoped to breed her with his pig 'Boar Scarloff'. More recently, Stephan Pastis created a character named 'Pig' in his syndicated strip *Pearls Before Swine*. 'Pig' is dim-witted but well meaning and has an awkward love of pork products. In Britain, David Sutherland developed a strip based on Dennis the Menace's pig named 'Rasher'. Rasher's family included his brother Hamlet, his sister Virginia Ham, Uncle Crackling and Little Piglet. Marvel Comics made fun of their own superhero Spider-Man in *Marvel Tails Starring Peter Porker, the Spectacular Spider-Ham*. More recently, the pig 'Harry Plopper' appeared as 'Spider-Pig' in *The Simpsons Movie*, with Homer singing a parody of the old Spider-Man theme song that asks 'can he swing, from a web? No he can't, he's a pig'.

Porky Pig was created by animator Bob Clampett and introduced in Friz Freleng's 1935 animated short *I Haven't Got a Hat*. Porky stole the show in this animal version of the *Our Gang* films and eventually became a star for Warner Brothers, ending the Looney Tunes shorts with his signature line 'Th-th-th-that's all folks!' Porky originally took his stutter from Joe Dougherty, the voice actor who played him. Mel Blanc, who took over the character's voice in 1937, kept the stutter, finding it suggestive of the grunting of actual pigs.[31]

Disney's 1933 Academy Award-winning short *Three Little Pigs* is one of the most famous animated films, one wildly popular with audiences, in part because it reflected the fears and aspirations of Americans living through the Great Depression. It brought the familiar story to life and introduced Frank Churchill's enduring song 'Who's Afraid of the Big Bad Wolf?' There were several sequels produced in the 1930s, and even more adaptations during the Second World War, including Disney's *The Thrifty Pig*, which gives the Big Bad Wolf a Nazi hat and swastika-emblazoned armband, and Tex Avery's 1942 MGM cartoon *Blitz Wolf*, in which 'Adolf Wolf' attempts to invade the state of 'Pigmania' before being stopped by 'Sgt Pork'.[32]

Pigs have not been as central to feature-length films, other than those adapted from children's literature. A notable early film about pigs is the strange 1907 Pathé short *Le Cochon Danseur*, in which a pig dressed in fancy clothes flirts with a girl, who in turn humiliates him, strips off his suit and compels him to dance for her. The pig costume is particularly wonderful, as is the puppetry at the end that makes the pig roll his eyes, flop his ears and stick out his tongue. Pigs have added comic elements to films and television programmes including the *Toy Story* films (which feature a pig named Hamm modelled after the Little Tikes' Piggy Bank), *College Road Trip*, *A Private Function* (a comedy about post-Second World War food rationing in England) and the late

Still from a 1907 silent film, *Le Cochon Danseur*.

Eddie Albert, Eva Gabor and Arnold Ziffel, the talented pig they treated like a son in the American television show *Green Acres*, 1965.

An M·G·M· CARTOON
BLITZ WOLF
A Metro-Goldwyn-Mayer PICTURE
Directed by
TEX AVERY
in
TECHNICOLOR

1960s television show *Green Acres*, which featured a trained pig named Arnold Ziffel. The most famous pig in popular culture, however, is Miss Piggy, a character from *The Muppet Show* and its related films. Miss Piggy became a major star in the 1980s, known for her complicated relationship with Kermit the Frog and her role as first mate on the *Swinetrek* in the sketch 'Pigs in Space'. Miss Piggy endorsed a perfume titled 'Moi' and published a book (*Miss Piggy's Guide to Life*, 1981) that became a bestseller. Among her pieces of advice, 'Beauty is in the eye of the beholder and it may be necessary from time to time to give a stupid or misinformed beholder a black eye.'[33]

Representations of non-anthropomorphized pigs have a long history. The oldest known illustration of a pig, a wild boar in motion, was painted in the cave of Altamira in Spain during the Upper Paleolithic period, approximately 14,000 years ago. Wild boar appear in the art of the ancient world, with many notable images attributed to the artist known as 'the Pig Painter',

Poster for *Blitz Wolf*, Tex Avery's 1942 anti-German parody of 'Three Little Pigs'.

'Pigs in Space', a recurring skit from *The Muppet Show* (1976–81).

who worked in Greece in the fifth century BCE. Pigs appeared in religious art and sculpture, including many wonderful carvings of 'ecclesiastical pigs' in fourteenth- to sixteenth-century churches. Pigs appear in drawings by Paulus Potter, Dürer, Rembrandt, Rubens and George Morland and in oil paintings by Thomas Gainsborough, including his charming *Girl with Pigs* at Castle Howard, Yorkshire, in which a young girl watches piglets drink milk. In contrast, Jean-François Millet's *Killing the Hog* depicts men attempting to drag a reluctant pig to its death. More imaginative is the Belgian symbolist artist Félicien Rops' coloured etching *Pornocrates* or *La Dame au cochon* of 1896, which depicts, in his words, a 'beautiful naked girl, clad only in black shoes and gloves in silk, leather and velvet . . . Wearing a blindfold, she walks on a marble stage, guided by a pig with a "golden tail" across a blue sky.'[34]

Images of pigs are more often used in less psychologically inflected ways. Many British taverns and pubs have names such as 'Pig and Whistle' and 'Boar's Head' that have led to commercially painted signs. Interestingly, there is no clear explanation for the origin of the phrase 'pig and whistle'. Some claim that it is related to *pige-washael*, an ancient salutation to Our Lady. Others see it related to 'piggin of wassail', with 'piggin' referring to a small pot and 'wassail' to a festive drink. In Scotland, it is said that 'pig' is a pot and 'whistle' petty cash. Alternatively, it may simply mean what it says and refer to a pig joyously dancing and playing music. At Five Ash Down in Sussex, the sign for the tavern 'The Pig and Butcher' shows, on one side, the pig begging for mercy, and on the other, the two enjoying each other's company after the butcher suffered a change of heart and spared the animal.[35]

Although pigs continue to be visually ubiquitous, especially in advertising, contemporary artists have represented them to

Jean-François Millet, *Killing the Hog*, 1867–70, pastel on canvas.

Thomas Gainsborough, *Girl with Pigs*, 1782, oil on canvas. During its exhibition a countryman remarked 'They be deadly like pigs, but nobody ever saw pigs feeding together but what one on 'em had a foot in the trough'.

comment upon the complex history of pigs and humans. Two themes are especially noteworthy: the return of pigs to urban spaces, and the interrogation of our lived relationship with pigs.

By the early twentieth century pigs had largely disappeared from modern cities, as urban pigs came to stand for poverty and slum conditions and as technology made it possible for pig farms and slaughtering operations to be located near points of production rather than consumption. Today, pigs generally only appear in the city as meat and as representations. This replacement of the real animal with its broken-down body or with representations in paint, fibreglass and bronze marks both the repression of the complex history of human–pig interactions and our radical distance from most non-human animals in late modernity.

A gargoyle in the form of a pig with bagpipes at Melrose Abbey in the Scottish Borders.

Where live pigs once were bought, sold and slaughtered, life-sized bronze piggy banks now stand. In the United States, Eric Berg's 'Philbert', the mascot of Philadelphia's Reading Terminal Market, and 'Rachel', who plays the same role at Seattle's Pike Place Market, appear in thousands of tourist photos and collect coins for food-oriented charities. They do not remind us of the real animal behind the meat, as does Louis Molina's bicycle rack located outside Los Angeles's Grand Central Market, which features a pair of pig heads cast in steel from ones originally purchased in the market. The absence of cuteness here contrasts with the recent vogue for decorated fibreglass pigs, which have taken over a number of cities in the wake of the pioneering CowParade held in Zurich in 1998. Cincinnati and Seattle have been filled with colourful and whimsical pig sculptures in recent years, while in Bath, England, the King Bladud's Pigs exhibition involved 105 decorated pig sculptures, all auctioned off to benefit a rails-to-trails project.[36]

While these projects are popular with the public, they represent what one critic has called 'a dumbing-down of culture'. These

Félicien Rops, *Pornocrates*, 1896, pastel drawing with watercolour.

exhibitions are fun, seldom drawing protests, as did artist Andrew
Leicester's *Cincinnati Gateway* project in the 1980s, which included bronzed flying pigs atop columns that symbolized the
millions of hogs that helped to build the city. The mayor of Cincinnati found the pigs an inappropriate symbol for his 'vision of a
modern metropolis', arguing that the sculptures 'would make
the city a laughingstock'. After extensive controversy, the pro-
pig forces prevailed. In the long run, Leicester's flying pigs were
a big hit, providing a sense of civic identity and belonging.[37]

Other visual arts are designed to provoke. British artist Damien
Hirst frequently uses animals in his sculptures, including a
whole pig sliced in half down the middle, and displayed in two
separate tanks. Using motorized pulleys, the two halves of the
pig endlessly pass each other, unable to remain whole. This work,
This Little Piggy Went to Market, This Little Piggy Stayed at Home
(1996), engendered controversy and prompted viewers to think
about life, death and the place of animals in art.

168

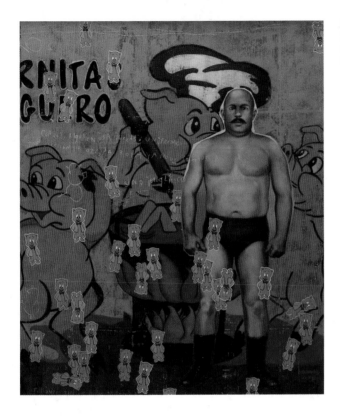

Armando Romero, *Pork Flakes (The Gladiator)*, 2006, oil on canvas.

Los Angeles artist Paul McCarthy has been using sculptures of pigs as part of 'an indictment of the greed and idiocy that conditioned the economic crisis'. His recent sculpture, *Mountain* (2009), is part of his ongoing Pig Island project, which 'is the orgiastic breeding ground for unnatural hybrids' of pigs and politicians that serve to critique American imperialism and gluttony.[38]

Other artists have used living or recently killed pigs in their work to question the boundaries between humans and animals.

Tattooed pigs at Belgian conceptual artist Wim Delvoye's 'Art Farm' in China, 2008.

The German artists Carsten Höller and Rosemarie Trockel's *Ein Haus für Schweine und Menschen* (A House for Pigs and People) gave a family of pigs the run of a house and yard at Documenta X in Germany in 1997, making them visible to people through a large sheet of glass. People could watch the pigs in the house, but not vice versa, reminding viewers of the ambivalence with which we view pigs and encouraging them to contemplate the boundaries between the human and the animal. In her 2008 performance *Inthewrongplaceness*, the artist Kira O'Reilly, naked, performed 'a 10-minute slow crushing dance with a sow carcass' that was repeated over the course of several hours. Her intimate yet unsensationalized relationship with the dead pig, investigating the similarities between the pig's body and her own, made a moving statement about both mortality and the deep, if unac-knowledged, connections between humans and pigs.[39]

These recent artistic uses of pigs foreground the alienation of many in the West from both modern society and the natural world. This critical thinking with pigs tends to emphasize human concerns, but as living animals, pigs can just as easily remind us of their uniqueness and agency as problematize our humanity.

8 The Return of the Repressed: Wild-living Pigs

Most pigs are largely invisible, raised in confinement, slaughtered behind factory walls and delivered to grocery stores, where consumers pick up their pork, ham and bacon in neat shrink-wrapped packages. But in a strange paradox, people are increasingly likely to come across signs of wild-living pigs, including feral domestic hogs, wild boar and mixes of the two. Feral pigs are considered one of the world's most troublesome invasive species because they root up native vegetation, destroy crops, spread weeds and disease, and eat juvenile tortoises, reptiles and birds.[1] They also remind us that pigs are not as completely under our control as we might like.

Feral pigs damage fields and golf courses, spread swine diseases, cause soil erosion and compete with native species for resources and habitat. According to the US Department of Agriculture (USDA), free-ranging populations of wild pigs exist in at least eighteen states. The total population in the United States is estimated at between 1 and 4 million pigs. A feral pig can cause $50,000 in damage to a golf course in one night and such pigs are blamed for $800 million in annual damages nationwide, even though the federal government spends less than $1 million in efforts to control these animals.[2]

Free-living pigs can be found in California, where feral pigs have existed since the early nineteenth century and wild boars

Boars from a
12th-century
English bestiary.

were first imported for hunting by a Monterey county landowner in the 1920s.[3] These highly adaptable animals average two litters per year in the conducive California climate, producing a total population estimated at more than 70,000. In California any feral pig is legal game and there is no bag limit or seasonal restriction, although pigs need to be tagged when killed. Despite these liberal regulations, which enable hunters to take around 30,000 wild pigs annually, wild hogs continue to increase in number and expand their range. Wild pigs are the most important big game animals in the state, with California the only state in the Lower 48 in which an animal other than deer tops the charts.[4]

Feral pigs are a particular threat to native plants and animals. The National Park Service has built a 32-mile-long fence around Pinnacles National Monument in California to prevent these non-native species from further invading the park. Off the California coast, an even larger effort cleared Santa Cruz Island of its wild pigs. Santa Cruz Island, the largest of the eight Channel Islands, lies just nineteen miles from the mainland. Sheep ranchers started using the island in the 1850s and brought pigs with them as farm animals. Pigs escaped, of course, and over time the domestic animals became a feral and extremely problematic invasive species, disrupting native plant life, spreading seeds of non-native plants and rooting through sites used by the Chumash, the earliest inhabitants of the island.

The pigs had a devastating effect on the Santa Cruz Island fox, a dwarf species found only on the Channel Islands. It was not that pigs and foxes were in direct competition. Instead, the availability of pigs as a food source transformed the ecology of the island, enabling golden eagles to colonize it. Once the golden eagles arrived, they found the cat-sized foxes to be easy prey. By 2004 there were fewer than 100 foxes left on Santa Cruz Island.

In 2004 the fox was classified as a federally protected endangered species. The National Park Service began a captive breeding programme for the foxes and began removing golden eagles from the island and reintroducing bald eagles, which do not feed on foxes or piglets. Most importantly, the NPS and the Nature Conservancy, which own the island jointly, initiated a $5 million project to eliminate the feral pigs, contracting with the New Zealand-based company Prohunt, Inc. to track down and destroy all of the island's pigs.

Activist groups, including In Defense of Animals and the Channel Islands Animal Protection Association, sought to stop the 'massacre' of pigs with lawsuits and appeals to the public, but to no avail. Between April 2005 and July 2006, 5,036 feral pigs were killed on the island. Toward the end of this effort, officials took advantage of the sociability of pigs by fitting one with a radio collar. This 'indicator pig' would then lead hunters to pigs on the island that they had missed. By late 2007, after extensive monitoring for stray swine, the project was declared a success. Early indications suggest that the pig eradication has made quite a difference. The fox population seems to be growing, bald eagles have been re-introduced and are nesting on the island for the first time in over 50 years and native plants like the coreopsis are blooming in record numbers.[5]

In the American South wild hogs are both hunted for sport and captured for use in hog-dog rodeos. In Texas the feral pig population is estimated at 1.5 million. Hired hunters have been brought in to control wild pigs there and in Nebraska, where the pigs have destroyed corn crops and have the potential to spread diseases to the state's hog farms.[6] The threat is not just to corporate hog farms but to humans as well. An *E. coli* outbreak in California in 2006 that killed three people and sickened hundreds was immediately linked to the consumption of contaminated raw spinach. Investigators now believe that feral pigs were the vectors that transferred the *E. coli* bacteria from the manure from a cattle feedlot to the spinach fields.[7]

In hog-dog rodeos wild hogs have been turned into a profitable, if contested, form of entertainment. In these events, a wild pig is prodded into the ring from a large pen full of hogs that have been captured the day before. The dogs are released and chase and corner the pig. Dogs are classified as either 'bay' dogs that only corner the hog or 'catch' dogs that bite and hold the hogs. The dogs are often regional breeds, like the Catahoula and Red Bone, which are judged for the quality of their skills in the ring. While in an actual hunt the dogs would bay the hog until the hunter arrived to shoot the pig, in the rodeos, the dogs are not allowed to bite or attack a hog. In fact, at the Ocmulgee Wild Hog Festival in southern Georgia, any dog that 'caught' a hog was quickly pried loose and disqualified from competition. The hogs, however, operate under no such restrictions, so most of the dogs are equipped with large collars made of bulletproof material that the boars cannot penetrate with their teeth or tusks. These defensive armaments are used in hunting as well, but even so, it is common for hunters to lose dogs to the ferocity of the wild hogs.

The major event on the circuit is Uncle Earl's Hog Dog Trials in Louisiana, first held in 1995. An entire industry has sprung

Wild hogs in a holding pen at the Ocmulgee Wild Hog Festival, Georgia.

up around baying and hog hunting, chronicled in the niche magazine *Bayed Solid*.[8] It is unclear how long this backcountry tradition will last, however. This subculture is increasingly suspicious of outsiders, well aware of growing opposition to their sport. The Humane Society of the United States (HSUS) sees these rodeos as 'barbarically cruel events that pit a trained attack dog against a defenseless hog that has had his tusks removed'. The HSUS has encouraged the prosecution of hog-dog rodeo promoters under animal cruelty statutes and, when not possible, the passage of new laws in the South banning the practice. Most laws, including one passed in Mississippi in early 2008, ban only hog-dog fighting, not those 'trials' where the hogs (and dogs for that matter) are not mutilated or killed.[9] The contestation over these events pits defenders of rural traditions against what they see as moralistic outsiders bent on further destroying local communities. Given the success of the animal welfare community thus far, it is perhaps best not to count on being able to see a 'baying contest' in a decade or so.

Southerners have also managed to turn wild hogs into celebrity animals. Outside the town of Brooks in Fayette County, Georgia, Bill Coursey shot what became known as the 'Brooks Beast,' a 500 kg (1,100 lb) wild boar, as it was eating plants and sod in his front yard. This pig was larger than the famed 'Hogzilla,' an 363 kg (800 lb) boar shot in southern Georgia. It was later discovered that the 'Brooks Beast' was a semi-feral hog that escaped from a nearby property. There have been other contenders for biggest feral pig. In fact, about once per year a new one emerges, most recently the 'Monster Pig' (522 kg or 1,150 lb) killed by an eleven-year-old boy in Alabama. As it turns out, this 'monster pig' came from a hog breeder and was sold to a hunting preserve where the kid shot it.[10]

Similar controversy stalked the original 'Hogzilla', shot in Alapaha, Georgia, in 2004. Originally alleged to be 3.7 metres (twelve feet) long and weighing over 450 kg (1,000 lb), the wild pig's remains were exhumed for an American television documentary, which suggested that it was between 2.1 and 2.7 metres (seven and nine feet) long and weighed only 363 kg (800 lb). DNA analysis revealed that Hogzilla was a hybrid of wild boar and domestic swine. Hogzilla and other big pigs reflect a long tradition of tall tales about hunting and the outdoors. Hogzilla is celebrated annually with a parade in Georgia and has given its name to both a bluegrass band and to the B-movie *The Legend of Hogzilla*.[11]

Feral pigs are problems in other parts of the world as well. The original British wild boar population became extinct over 300 years ago, and for hundreds of years wild boar were only seen in zoos and nature preserves. Escapes and deliberate releases of wild boar from farming operations have resulted in three known

English breeding populations of wild-living pigs: near the Kent and East Sussex border, in west Dorset and in the Forest of Dean in Gloucestershire. While the total population is still small – estimated at no more than several thousand animals – it is likely that wild-living pigs will become established through much of England in the next several decades. The Department for Environment, Food and Rural Affairs (DEFRA) has decided to leave the management of these animals to local communities and individual landowners, at least for the moment. Non-governmental groups, like the British Wild Boar Organization, collect and chart wild boar and feral pig sightings, including a growing number of unwelcome confrontations between these pigs and humans and destruction of property.[12]

The situation is much worse in Australia, where there are an estimated 23 million wild pigs, concentrated in New South Wales and Queensland. These animals have caused extensive and expensive damage to sugar cane and banana crops, preyed upon lambs, goats and native animals, and contaminated streams and rivers. Authorities are especially concerned that Australia's

Butchering a pig – December, in a calendar in a Book of Hours, c. 1440.

Gustave Courbet,
A Pig's Head, 1869,
oil on canvas.

feral pigs could serve as vectors for diseases, particularly foot-and-mouth disease, that might devastate commercial pig operations or, in the worst case, spread to humans and other domestic animals. To control these wild animals, feral pigs are poisoned (using a bait called PIGOUT), trapped and shot from the ground and from the air by professional hunters (one company is called Boar Busters). While there is some recreational hunting and commercial harvesting of wild-living pigs that benefits some communities, wild-living pigs pose challenges to humans, other animals and the environment that will only continue to grow in Australia and elsewhere.[13]

The presence of wild-living pigs throughout the globe should be seen as an encouraging sign, a reminder that these highly

Hog at a fence,
Minnesota.

adaptable, intelligent and social animals will never be fully
controlled by humans. Even the hunting of wild boar and feral
pigs recalls earlier human interactions with *Sus scrofa*, an animal that has had an impact on human life and culture for
thousands of years. In the long and complicated history of the
human–pig relationship, pigs have been praised and condemned, an ambivalence fundamentally related to the central
fact of this cross-species interaction: humans kill pigs for food.
Hundreds of millions of pigs are slaughtered each year for
human consumption, killing enabled by both the nostalgic
and anthropomorphized images of pigs and the distance the
modern meat industry has created between pigs and pork. In
making this bloodshed possible, we have underestimated the

pig, condemned this animal for its supposedly inferior form and talents, although these are almost always measured by human standards. While it is unlikely that most people will start to think differently, and more importantly, choose a different lived relationship with pigs, we could at least try to appreciate what one astute scholar of the pig termed 'hogritude': the practical condition and mythical essence of just being a pig.[14] An effort to understand the pig and its pigness just might begin to remove the ambivalence from our attitudes about and practices towards pigs, narrowing, if only slightly, a gap between humans and pigs that reflects the devaluation of life itself.

Timeline of the Pig

c. 14,000 BCE	c. 9,000 BCE	c. 5,000 BCE	c. 450 BCE	c. 100 CE
Oldest known illustration of a pig, a wild boar in motion, was painted in a cave at Altamira, Spain	Wild boar are domesticated in Eastern Turkey and China	Pig breeding is well established in China	The Book of Leviticus codifies the exclusion of pigs from those animals that are good to eat	Plutarch's *Gryllus* suggests that it is better to be a pig than to be a human

Entelodont
Dinohyus

1820s–1830s	1826–1832	1847	1865
Cincinnati, Ohio becomes 'Porkopolis,' the centre of American pork production	Hog cart riots occur periodically in New York City as part of the larger struggle between city officials and pig owners	William Youatt publishes *The Pig: A Treatise on the Breeds, Management, Feeding, and Medical Treatment of Swine*, the first synthetic treatment of the pig	The Union Stock Yard & Transit Co. is established in Chicago, making it the 'hog butcher for the world' for decades

1933	1936	1937	1945	1952
Disney's animated short *Three Little Pigs* creates an enduring version of the fairy tale	Smithfield Foods, which will become the world's largest pork producer and processor, is founded in Virginia by Joseph W. Luter, Sr	Hormel Foods introduces Spam	George Orwell publishes *Animal Farm*, in which 'all animals are equal, but some animals are more equal than others'	E. B. White publishes *Charlotte's Web*

| 1492–1550 | c. 1600 | 1805 | 1821 | 1823 |

Pigs expand rapidly in the 'new world' in the wake of the Columbian Exchange

Indigenous people in the Caribbean show European colonists how to cook pigs on a wooden platform resting on sticks called a 'barabicu', giving the world a great culinary tradition

William Frederick Pinchbeck explains how to train a 'learned pig' in *The Expositor, or Many Mysteries Unravelled*

Charles Lamb publishes 'A Dissertation Upon Roast Pork' in *The London Magazine*

The first Berkshire hogs are brought to the United States from Britain

| c. 1870 | 1884 | 1906 | 1916 | 1926 |

German immigrant Charles Feltman begins selling sausages in rolls at Coney Island, paving the way for the hot dog

The National Pig Breeders Association is formed in Britain

Upton Sinclair's *The Jungle* makes Americans wary about their meat, leading to industry reform and government regulation

Clarence Saunders founds Piggly Wiggly, the first true self-service grocery store, in Memphis, Tennessee

Piglet appears in A. A. Milne's *Winnie the Pooh*

| early 1980s | 1992 | 1994 | 1995 | 2004–10 |

The eradication of the 'Creole Pig' begins in Haiti, while Vietnamese pot bellied pigs become fashionable pets in the United States

Smithfield opens its Tar Heel, North Carolina meat processing plant, the world's largest, capable of butchering over 32,000 pigs per day

Bill Niman begins selling antibiotic- and hormone-free pork from animals raised on family farms in Iowa

Babe, the film adaptation of Dick King-Smith's *The Sheep Pig* (1983), is a critical and popular success

Gestation crates used in intensive pig farming are banned or begin to be phased out in some US states, EU nations and New Zealand

References

PREFACE

1 Susan Hopmans, *The Great Murals of Farmer John Brand, Clougherty Meat Packing Co. in Vernon, California*, photographed by Peter Kenner (New York, 1971).
2 Sue Coe, *Dead Meat* (New York and London, 1996), pp. 87–8.

1 WHAT IS A PIG?

1 Draw a Pig, online at http://drawapig.desktopcreatures.com (accessed 30 September 2009).
2 Lyall Watson, *The Whole Hog: Exploring the Extraordinary Potential of Pigs* (Washington, DC, 2004), pp. 27–8; Spencer G. Lucas and Robert J. Emry, 'Taxonomy and Biochronological Significance of *Paraentelodon*, a Giant Entelodont from the Late Oligocene of Eurasia', *Journal of Vertebrate Paleontology*, XIX/1 (March 1999), pp. 160–68.
3 Umberto Albarella, Keith Dobney, Anton Ervynck and Peter Rowley-Conwy, *Pigs and Humans: 10,000 Years of Interaction* (Oxford, 2007), pp. 1–12.
4 Watson, *The Whole Hog*, pp. 99, 92.
5 Albarella et al., *Pigs and Humans*, pp. 1–12.
6 Watson, *The Whole Hog*, p. 99.
7 See Valerie Porter, *Pigs: A Handbook to the Breeds of the World*, illustrated by Jake Tebbit (nr Robertsbridge, East Sussex, 1993), pp. 13–17 for an overview.
8 Greger Larson et al., 'Ancient DNA, Pig Domestication, and the

Spread of the Neolithic into Europe', *Proceedings of the National Academy of Sciences*, 13 September 2007, online at www.pnas.org/content/104/39/15276.abstract; 'Pigs Domesticated "Many Times"', *BBC News*, 11 March 2005, online at http://news.bbc.co.uk/2/hi/science/nature/4337435.stm; Liz Seward, 'Pig DNA Reveals Farming History', *BBC News*, 4 September 2007, online at http://news.bbc.co.uk/2/hi/science/nature/6978203.stm. (all sites accessed 30 September 2009).

9 Sarah M. Nelson, ed., *Ancestors for the Pigs: Pigs in Prehistory* (Philadelphia, PA, 1998), p. 101; Edward Cody, 'Oh, to be Born in the Year of the Pig', *Washington Post*, 1 March 2007.

10 Porter, *Pigs*, pp. 175–6; Sigrid Schmalzer, 'Breeding a Better China: Pigs, Practices, and Place in a Chinese County, 1929–1937', *Geographical Review*, XCII/1 (January 2002), pp. 1–22.

11 Porter, *Pigs*, p. 91.

12 Julian Wiseman, *The Pig: A British History* (London, 2000), pp. 47–52; Porter, *Pigs*, pp. 79, 106–7.

13 British Pig Association, online at www.britishpigs.org.uk (accessed 30 September 2009); James Buchan, 'My Hogs', *London Review of Books*, XXIII/20 (18 October 2001), pp. 30–31.

14 Robert E. F. Smith and David Christian, *Bread and Salt: A Social and Economic History of Food and Drink in Russia* (Cambridge, 1984), pp. 327–8; Porter, *Pigs*, pp. 161–9.

15 Ibid., pp. 231–2; 236–7.

2 A SHARED HISTORY

1 Jane C. Goodale, *To Sing With Pigs is Human: The Concept of Person in Papua New Guinea* (Seattle and London, 1995), p. 250.

2 Peter D. Dwyer and Monica Minnegal, 'Person, Place or Pig: Animal Attachments and Human Transactions in New Guinea', in *Animals in Person: Cultural Perspectives on Human-Animal Intimacies*, ed. J. Knight (Oxford and New York, 2005), pp. 37–60.

3 Goodale, *To Sing With Pigs is Human*, p. 250.

4 William F. S. Miles, 'Pigs, Politics and Social Change in Vanuatu', *Society and Animals*, v/2 (1997); Kirk Huffman, 'Pigs, Prestige and Copyright in the Western Pacific', *Explore*, xxix/6 (February 2008), p. 25.

5 Umberto Albarella, Keith Dobney, Anton Ervynck and Peter Rowley-Conwy, *Pigs and Humans: 10,000 Years of Interaction* (Oxford, 2007), pp. 1–12.

6 Richard A. Lobban, Jr, 'Pigs and their Prohibition', *International Journal of Middle East Studies*, xxvi/1 (1994), pp. 57–75.

7 Marvin Harris, *The Sacred Cow and the Abominable Pig: Riddles of Food and Culture* (New York, 1987).

8 Richard C. Foltz, *Animals in Islamic Tradition and Muslim Cultures* (Oxford, 2006), p. 131.

9 'Hog Wild in Athens bce! Role of Pigs in Social and Religious Life Provides Insights into Ancient Greece', online at www.buffalo.edu/news/4837 (accessed 29 September 2009).

10 J.M.C. Toynbee, *Animals in Roman Life and Art* (London, 1973), pp. 15–16.

11 Plutarch, 'Odysseus and Gryllus', in *Moral Essays*, trans. with an introduction by Rex Warner, notes by D. A. Russell (Harmondsworth, 1971), pp. 161–3.

12 Caius Plinius Secundus, *Pliny's Natural History: A Selection from Philemon Holland's Translation* (Oxford, 1964), pp. 81–2.

13 Boria Sax, *Animals in the Third Reich: Pets, Scapegoats, and the Holocaust* (New York and London, 2000), pp. 64–5.

14 Luke 15:11–32; Matthew 8:30–32 (cf. Mark 5:11–13 and Luke 8:32–3).

15 David Salter, *Holy and Noble Beasts: Encounters with Animals in Medieval Literature* (Cambridge, 2001), p. 45.

16 Peter Stallybrass and Allon White, *The Poetics and Politics of Transgression* (Ithaca, NY, 1986), p. 51; Mitchell B. Merback, *The Thief, the Cross, and the Wheel: Pain and the Spectacle of Punishment in Medieval and Renaissance Europe* (London, 1998), pp. 188–9.

17 Sax, *Animals in the Third Reich*, p. 71.

18 Linda Kalof, *Looking at Animals in Human History* (London, 2007), p. 64.

19 E. P. Evans, *The Criminal Prosecution and Capital Punishment of Animals* [1906] (London and Boston, MA, 1988), quotation from the foreword by Nicholas Humphrey; Darren Oldridge, *Strange Histories: The Trial of the Pig, the Walking Dead, and Other Matters of Fact from the Medieval and Renaissance Worlds* (London and New York, 2005).

3 HOGS IN THE NEW WORLD

1 Alfred W. Crosby, *The Columbian Exchange: Biological and Cultural Consequences of 1492* (Westport, CT, 1972), p. 75.
2 Ibid., pp. 76, 78–9.
3 Valerie Porter, *Pigs: A Handbook to the Breeds of the World*, illustrated by Jake Tebbit (nr Robertsbridge, East Sussex, 1993), p. 214.
4 Alfred W. Crosby, *Ecological Imperialism: The Biological Expansion of Europe, 900–1900* (Cambridge and New York, 1986), pp. 176–8, 230.
5 William Cronon, *Changes in the Land: Indians, Colonists, and the Ecology of New England* (New York, 1983), p. 201.
6 Ibid., pp. 135–7.
7 Cited in S. Jonathan Bass, '"How 'Bout a Hand for the Hog": The Enduring Nature of the Swine as a Cultural Symbol in the South', *Southern Cultures*, I/3 (Spring 1995), p. 301.
8 See Albert Matthews, 'Uncle Sam', *Proceedings of the American Antiquarian Society*, XXIX (Worcester, MA, 1909), pp. 21–65, esp. 48–9.
9 David Grettler, 'Environmental Change and Conflict over Hogs in Early Nineteenth-Century Delaware', *Journal of the Early Republic*, XIX/2 (1999), pp. 197–220.
10 Cited in Bass, '"How 'Bout a Hand for the Hog"', p. 304.
11 Indiana Historical Bureau, 'Hoosier Hogs' (1994), online at www.in.gov/history/files/7027.pdf (accessed 30 September 2009).
12 Margaret Walsh, *The Rise of the Midwestern Meat Packing Industry* (Lexington, KY, 1982).

13 See Steven J. Ross, *Workers on the Edge: Work, Leisure, and Politics in Industrializing Cincinnati, 1788–1890* (New York, 1985).

14 Frederick Law Olmsted, *A Journey Through Texas; or, A Saddle-Trip on the Southwestern Frontier: with a Statistical Appendix* (New York, 1857), p. 9.

15 Frances Trollope, *The Domestic Manners of the Americans* [1832] (New York, 1960), pp. 88–9.

16 Margaret Walsh, 'From Pork Merchant to Meat Packer: The Midwestern Meat Industry in the Mid-Nineteenth Century', *Agricultural History*, LVI/1 (1982), pp. 127–37; William Cronon, *Nature's Metropolis: Chicago and the Great West* (New York, 1992).

17 John Duffy, *The History of Public Health in New York City, 1625–1866* (New York, 1968), pp. 216–18; Hendrick Hartog, 'Pigs and Positivism', *Wisconsin Law Review* (July/August 1985).

18 Charles Dickens, *American Notes for General Circulation* (New York, 1868), p. 38; Frederick Law Olmsted, *Passages in the Life of an Unpractical Man* [1857], in *Writing New York: A Literary Anthology*, ed. Phillip Lopate (New York, 2000), p. 249.

19 Duffy, *The History of Public Health in New York City*, pp. 383–6. See also Brett Mizelle, 'The Disappearance (and Slight Return) of Pigs in American Cities', *Antennae*, XII (Spring 2010), pp. 79–85.

20 Cited in Bass, '"How 'Bout a Hand for the Hog"', p. 308.

21 Eliot Wigginton, *The Foxfire Book* (New York, 1972), pp. 189–207.

22 Peter Kaminsky, *Pig Perfect: Encounters with Remarkable Swine and Some Great Ways to Cook Them* (New York, 2005), pp. 13–23; James Villas, 'Cry, The Beloved Country Ham', in *American Taste: A Celebration of Gastronomy Coast-to-Coast* (New York, 1982), pp. 287–93.

23 Ferrol Sams, *Run with the Horsemen* (New York, 1982), p. 81.

24 Harry Crews, *A Childhood: The Biography of a Place* (New York, 1978).

25 Cited in Ted Ownby, *Subduing Satan: Religion, Recreation, and Manhood in the Rural South, 1865–1920* (Chapel Hill, NC, 1990), p. 93.

26 John Kessler, 'Going Whole Hog', *Atlanta Journal and Constitution*, 23 March 2008.

1 Christopher G. Davis and Biing-Hwan Lin, 'Factors Affecting U.S. Pork Consumption', USDA Economic Research Service, Report LDP-M–130-01 (May 2005), pp. 1–18.

2 *The Simpsons*, 'Lisa the Vegetarian', episode 3F13, written by David S. Cohen, directed by Mark Kirkland, originally aired 15 October 1995; Michael Pollan, *The Omnivore's Dilemma: A Natural History of Four Meals* (New York, 2006), p. 318.

3 Davis and Lin 'Factors Affecting US Pork Consumption', pp. 6–7, 10–11.

4 John S. Wilson, 'Health Department', *Godey's Lady's Book*, 60 (February 1860), p. 178.

5 Thomas Farrington De Voe, *The Market Assistant: Containing a Brief Description of Every Article of Human Food Sold in the Public Markets of the Cities of New York, Boston, Philadelphia, and Brooklyn* (New York, 1867), p. 78.

6 Roger Horowitz, *Putting Meat on the American Table: Taste, Technology, Transformation* (Baltimore and London, 2005), p. 45.

7 Ibid., pp. 59–62.

8 Ibid., pp. 63, 69; Daniel Defoe, *A Tour Through the Whole Island of Great Britain* (1724–1726), ed. P. N. Furbank, W. R. Owens and A. J. Coulson (New Haven, CT, 1991), p. 123.

9 Horowitz, *Putting Meat on the American Table*, pp. 78–82, 91–100.

10 Ibid., pp. 69, 73.

11 Dan Armstrong and Dustin Black, *The Book of Spam: A Most Glorious and Definitive Compendium of the World's Favorite Canned Meat* (New York, 2007); Hormel's official site is www.spam.com.

12 Steve W. Martinez, 'Vertical Coordination in the Pork and Broiler Industries: Implications for Pork and Chicken Products', Economic Research Service, US Department of Agriculture, Report No. 777 (April 1999), p. 26.

13 Upton Sinclair, *The Jungle* [1906] (New York, 1920), pp. 47, 40–41.

14 Marco D'Eramo, *The Pig and the Skyscraper: Chicago: A History of Our Future*, trans. Graeme Thomson, foreword by Mike Davis (London, 2002), pp. 32–3.

15 Mike Freeman, 'Clarence Saunders: The Piggly Wiggly Man', *Tennessee Historical Quarterly* (Spring 1992), pp. 161–9.

16 Jeff Tietz, 'Boss Hog', *Rolling Stone*, 14 December 2006, online at www.rollingstone.com/news/story/21727641/boss_hog/ (accessed 28 September 2009); Mary Hendrickson and William Heffernan, 'Concentration of Animal Markets, April 2007', online at www.nfu.org/wp-content/2007-heffernanreport.pdf (accessed 30 September 2009).

17 Nathanael Johnson, 'Swine of the Times: The Making of the Modern Pig', *Harper's Magazine* (May 2006), pp. 47–56, quotation on p. 50.

18 Ibid., pp. 52–3; Jon Mooallem, 'Carnivores, Capitalists, and the Meat We Read', *The Believer* (October 2005), online at www.believermag.com/issues/200510/ (accessed 28 September 2009).

19 Mark Honeyman and Mike Duffy, 'Iowa's Changing Swine Industry: A Look at the Past 25 Years', *Iowa State University Animal Industry Report 2006*, online at www.thepigsite.com/articles/2/ai-genetics-reproduction/1714/iowas-changing-swine-industry (accessed 28 September 2009); 'It Isn't Easy Being Pork Queen if Iowa Turns Cold Shoulder', *Wall Street Journal*, 6 June 2005.

20 Richard Curtis Lacy, 'Hogs', *The New Georgia Encyclopedia*, online at www.georgiaencyclopedia.org/nge/Article.jsp?id=h–2100andhl=y (accessed 30 September 2009).

21 David Cecelski and Mary Lee Kerr, 'Hog Wild: How Corporate Hog Operations Are Slaughtering Family Farms and Poisoning the Rural South', *Southern Exposure*, XXII/3 (Fall 1992), pp. 8–15. The North Carolina *News and Observer* won the 1996 Pulitzer Prize for its five-part series on North Carolina's 'pork revolution', online at www.pulitzer.org/archives/5892 (accessed 30 September 2009).

22 John R. Moore, 'Swine Production: A Global Perspective' (n.d.), online at en.engormix.com/MA-pig-industry/articles/swine-

production-global-perspective_124.htm (accessed 24 June 2010); Suzanne Deutsch, 'Smithfield Draws Mixed Reviews in Poland', *National Hog Farmer*, 15 July 2005.

23 Moore, 'Swine Production: A Global Perspective'; C. A. Tisdall and C. Wilson, 'Genetic Selection of Livestock and Economic Development', in *Economics and Ecology in Agriculture and Marine Production: Bioeconomics and Resource Use* (Cheltenham, 2003), pp. 140–50.

24 Jimin Wang and Hongbo Xiao, 'Development of the Hog Industry and its Integration in China', in *Pork Production in China: A Survey and Analysis of the Industry at a Lewis Turning Point*, ed. Jimin Wang and Mariko Watanabe (Chiba, Japan, 2008), pp. 1–30; Ruojan Wang, 'China – Pork Powerhouse of the World', in *Advances in Pork Production*, 17 (2006), pp. 33–46.

25 Johnson, 'Swine of the Times'.

26 Ibid., p. 54.

27 Ibid., p. 55.

28 Horowitz, *Putting Meat on the American Table*, pp. 68–9.

29 Charlie LeDuff, 'At a Slaughterhouse, Some Things Never Die', *New York Times*, 16 June 2000, reprinted in *Zoontologies: The Question of the Animal*, ed. Cary Wolfe (Minneapolis, MN, 2003), pp. 183–97; Tietz, 'Boss Hog'. See also Richard P. Horwitz, *Hog Ties: Pigs, Manure, and Mortality in American Culture* (New York, 1998).

30 Environmental Defense, 'Factory Hog Farming: The Big Picture', November 2000, online at www.edf.org/documents/2563_FactoryHogFarmingBigPicture.pdf (accessed 30 September 2009); Carolyn Johnsen, *Raising a Stink: The Struggle over Factory Hog Farms in Nebraska* (Lincoln and London, 2003); Tietz, 'Boss Hog'.

31 Johnsen, *Raising a Stink*, pp. 21–6; Ken Midkiff, *The Meat You Eat: How Corporate Farming has Endangered America's Food Supply* (New York, 2004), pp. 43–64; Gilbert R. Hollis and Stanley E. Curtis, 'General Characteristics of the US Swine Industry', in *Swine Nutrition*, ed. A. J. Lewis and L. L. Southern (Boca Raton, FL, 2001), p. 23.

32 Johnson, 'Swine of the Times', p. 56, quoting Paul Willis, a Niman Ranch farmer. Niman Ranch Pork is online at www.nimanranch.com/pork.aspx.

33 Peter Kaminsky, *Pig Perfect: Encounters with Remarkable Swine and Some Great Ways to Cook Them* (New York, 2005).

34 Anna Salewska, 'The Next Big Pig', *Toronto Globe and Mail*, 5 November 2008, pp. L1, L3.

35 Carla Emery, *The Encyclopedia of Country Living: An Old Fashioned Recipe Book* (Seattle, WA, 2003), pp. 837–63; Katie Zezima, 'Push to Eat Local Food is Hampered by Shortage', *New York Times*, 26 March 2010.

36 James Buchan, 'My Hogs', *London Review of Books*, 23.20 (18 October 2001), pp. 30–31.

37 R. W. Apple, Jr, 'A Prince of Pork: In Seattle, Recreating the Perfect Ham', *New York Times*, 17 May 2006.

38 Sarah Karnasiewicz, 'Going Whole Hog', Salon.com, 1 May 2007, online at www.salon.com/mwt/food/eat_drink/2007/05/01/pork_review/ (accessed 29 September 2009); Mooallem, 'Carnivores, Capitalists, and the Meat We Read'.

39 Pollan, *The Omnivore's Dilemma*, pp. 277, 410.

40 Cited in Nicolette Hahn Niman, 'Pig Out', *New York Times*, 14 March 2007; Peter Singer and Jim Mason, *The Way We Eat: Why Our Food Choices Matter* (New York, 2006), pp. 46–7.

41 Humane Society of the United States, 'Election '06: Animals Win In Arizona and Michigan', 7 November 2006, online at www.hsus.org/legislation_laws/ballot_initiatives/election_06_animals_win_.html (accessed 3 March 2010); Tracie Cone, 'California Lawmakers Rally Around Animal Welfare Issues', *San Jose Mercury News*, 29 May 2009.

5 HUMAN–PIG PARTNERSHIPS

1 Memorial University, Newfoundland, *Gazette*, 13 March 2008; Indiana Historical Bureau, 'Hoosier Hogs' (1994), online at www.in.gov/history/files/7027.pdf (accessed 30 September 2009).

2 Walter Sullivan, 'Truffles: Why Pigs Can Sniff Them Out', *New York Times*, 24 March 1982, online at www.nytimes.com/1982/03/24/garden/truffles-why-pigs-can-sniff-them-out.html (accessed 30 September 2009); Ian R. Hall, Gordon T. Brown and Alessandra Aambonelli, *Taming the Truffle: The History, Lore, and Science of the Ultimate Mushroom* (Portland, OR, 2007), pp. 204–5; 18–20.

3 William Bingley, *Memoirs of British Quadrupeds* (London, 1809), pp. 452–4.

4 Jeannette Townsend, 'Pigs: A Demining Tool of the Future?', *Journal of Mine Action*, VII/3 (December 2003), online at maic.jmu.edu/Journal/7.3/focus/townsend2/townsend2.htm (accessed 30 September 2009).

5 Peter Stallybrass and Allon White, *The Politics and Poetics of Transgression* (Ithaca, NY, 1986), pp. 58–9.

6 Ricky Jay, *Learned Pigs and Fireproof Women* (New York, 1987); Fleur Adcock and Jacqueline Simms, eds, *The Oxford Book of Creatures* (Oxford and New York, 1995), p. 6.

7 Brett Mizelle, '"I Have Brought My Pig to a Fine Market": Animals, Their Exhibitors, and Market Culture in the Early Republic', in *Cultural Change and the Market Revolution in America, 1789–1860*, ed. Scott C. Martin (Lanham, MD, 2005), pp. 181–216.

8 William Frederick Pinchbeck, *The Expositor; or, Many Mysteries Unravelled* (Boston, MA, 1805), pp. 26–7.

9 Jay, *Learned Pigs and Fireproof Women*, pp. 19–23.

10 Thomas Hood, 'The Lament of Toby, the Learned Pig', in *The Works of Thomas Hood, Comic and Serious, in Prose and Verse, with All the Original Illustrations*, ed. Tom Hood and Frances Freeling Hood Broderip (London, 1882), vol. II, pp. 348–51.

11 David Carlyon, *Dan Rice: The Most Famous Man You've Never Heard Of* (New York, 2004); Charles Philip Fox, *American Circus Posters* (New York, 1978).

12 Paul Erickson, 'Requiem for a Pig', unpublished paper in author's possession; Claire Osborn, 'Diving pig dies at Rodeo.

Electrocution investigated', Austin, Texas, *American Statesman*,
18 March 2005.

13 Valentine's Performing Pigs, online at www.valentinesperform
ingpigs.com/ (accessed 30 September 2009).

14 See for example Hedrick's Promotions, online at
www.hedricks.com/ and All-Alaskan Racing Pigs, online at
www.pigrace.com/ (both accessed 30 September 2009).

15 Julian Wiseman, *The Pig: A British History* (London, 2000), p. 62;
Elspeth Moncrieff, with Stephen and Iona Joseph, *Farm Animal
Portraits* (Woodbridge, Suffolk, 1997), p. 241.

16 'Big Norm, the World's Largest Pig, Dies', Syracuse, New York
Post-Standard, 13 September 2008.

17 Maev Kennedy, 'Museum Honors Dogs – and Ferrets – of War',
Guardian Unlimited, 13 July 2006, online at
arts.guardian.co.uk/news/story/0,,1819697,00.html (accessed
30 September 2009).

18 Sy Montgomery, *The Good Good Pig: The Extraordinary Life of
Christopher Hogwood* (New York, 2006).

19 Kathleen Myers, *The Complete Guide for the Care and Training of
Pet Potbellied Pigs* (New York, 2007), pp. 1–3.

20 Philip Dawdy, 'Judy Woods Gives Pigs a Place to Call Their Own',
The Seattle Times, 17 August 2008, online at
seattletimes.nwsource.com/html/pacificnw/2008111678_
pacificpigs17.html (accessed 30 September 2009).

21 'Pint-sized I pigs face extinction as crossbreeds crowd the meat
market', *The Pig Site*, 13 March 2007, online at
www.thepigsite.com/swinenews/13671/pintsized-i-pigs-face-
extinction-as-crossbreeds-crowd-the-meat-market (accessed
28 September 2009).

22 United States National Library of Medicine, National Institutes of
Health, 'Animals as Cold Warriors: Missiles, Medicine, and Man's
Best Friend', online at www.nlm.nih.gov/exhibition/animals/
atomic.html (accessed 30 September 2009).

23 C. J. Chivers, 'Tending a Fallen Marine, With Skill, Prayer and
Fury', *New York Times*, 2 November 2006, online at www.nytimes.

com/2006/11/02/world/middleeast/02medic.html (accessed 24
January 2007); Humane Society of the United States, 'Military
Uses Pigs in Trauma Training', www.hsus.org/animals_in_
research/animals_in_research_news/military_uses_pigs.html,
accessed 24 January 2007).

24 An Ravelingien, 'Use of Pigs for Xenotransplantation: The
Speciesism by Proxy Syndrome', *Xenotransplantation*, XII/3
(2005), pp. 235–9.

25 Richard Twyman, 'Genetic Modification of Pigs for Xenotransplantation', online at genome.wellcome.ac.uk/doc_WTD020910.
html (accessed 30 September 2009); 'Researchers Give Pigs Inner
Glow', *Los Angeles Times*, 14 January 2006, p. A10; Massie Santos
Ballon, 'Revisiting the Pigs', Manila, Philippines *Inquirer*, online at
showbizandstyle.inquirer.net/lifestyle/lifestyle/view/20070901–
85934/Revisiting_the_pigs (accessed 30 September 2009).

26 Adam Pick, 'Adverse Effects of Pig Valves', online at www.heart-
valve-surgery.com/heart-surgery-blog/?p=92 (accessed 10 March
2010).

27 'Ask Rabbi Lerner', online at judaism.about.com/library/
3_askrabbi_c/bl_pigs.htm (accessed 30 September 2009);
Randy Cohen, 'Pork: The Other White Medicine', *New York Times
Magazine*, 23 August 2009, p. 22

28 Jonathan L. Clark, 'Greening the Factory Farm: Toward a Theory
of Agri-Environmental Technoscience', PhD diss., Pennsylvania
State University (2010), p. 222; Susan McHugh, 'Clever Pigs,
Failing Piggeries', *Antennae*, XII (Spring 2010), pp. 23–4.

29 Gina Kolata, 'Cloning May Lead to Healthy Pork', *New York Times*,
27 March 2006, online at www.nytimes.com/2006/03/27/
health/27pig.html (accessed 30 September 2009); *The Daily
Show with Jon Stewart* (Comedy Central television programme),
29 March 2006.

30 Jeffery K. Taubenberger and David M. Morens, '1918 Influenza:
The Mother of All Pandemics', *Emerging Infectious Diseases*, XII/1
(January 2006), pp. 15–22; Joel C. Gaydos, Franklin H. Top Jr,
Richard A. Hodder and Philip K. Russell, 'Swine Influenza A

Outbreak, Fort Dix, New Jersey, 1976', *Emerging Infectious Diseases*, xii/1 (January 2006), pp. 23–8.

31 Debora MacKenzie, 'Pork Industry is Blurring the Science of Swine Flu', *New Scientist*, 30 April 2009, online at www.newscientist. com/blogs/shortsharpscience/2009/04/why-the-pork-industry-hates-th.html (accessed 3 March 2010).

32 Andrew Martin and Clifford Kraus, 'Pork Industry Fights Concerns Over Swine Flu', *New York Times*, 28 April 2009, online at www.nytimes.com/2009/04/29/business/economy/29trade.html (accessed 28 September 2009).

33 'Pigs at Risk from People as New Flu Spreads', *Reuters*, 9 July 2009, online at www.reuters.com/article/scienceNews/idUSTRE5687MZ20090709 (accessed 30 September 2009); 'Second Pseudorabies-Infected Swine Herd Found in Clark County', *Wisconsin Agriculturalist*, 25 April 2007, online at wisconsinagriculturist.com/story.aspx?s=11608andc=9 (accessed 30 September 2009); Nathanael Johnson, 'Swine of the Times: The Making of the Modern Pig', *Harper's Magazine* (May 2006), p. 49.

34 Alan Zarembo and Karen Kaplan, 'Flu? Don't Blame the Pig', *Los Angeles Times*, 9 May 2009, online at articles.latimes.com/2009/may/09/science/sci-swine-pigs9 (accessed 10 May 2009); Felicity Lawrence, 'The Pig's Revenge', *The Guardian*, 2 May 2009, online at www.guardian.co.uk/world/2009/may/02/swine-flu-pandemic-mexico-pig-farming (accessed 3 May 2009); Mike Davis, 'The Swine Flu Crisis Lays Bare the Meat Industry's Monstrous Power', *The Guardian*, 27 April 2009, online at www.guardian.co.uk/commentisfree/2009/apr/27/swine-flu-mexico-health (accessed 28 April 2009).

35 Nicholas D. Kristof, 'Our Pigs, Our Food, Our Health', and 'Pathogens in our Pork', *New York Times*, 12 March and 15 March 2009.

36 Golnar Motevalli, 'Afghanistan's Only Pig Quarantined in Flu Fear', *Reuters*, 5 May 2009, online at www.reuters.com/article/lifestyleMolt/idUSTRE5444XQ20090505 (accessed 30 September

2009); Robert Mackey, 'Quarantine for Afghanistan's Only Pig', *New York Times News Blog*, 8 May 2009, online at thelede.blogs. nytimes.com/2009/05/08/quarantine-for-afghanistans-only-pig/ (accessed 30 September 2009).

37 Nadim Audi, 'Culling Pigs in Flu Fight, Egypt Angers Herders and Dismays UN', *New York Times*, 1 May 2009; Michael Slackman, 'Belatedly, Egypt Spots Flaws in Wiping Out Pigs', *New York Times*, 20 September 2009.

6 GOOD PIGS AND BAD PIGS

1 John Berger, 'Why Look at Animals', *About Looking* (New York, 1980), p. 5; John Berger, 'Animal World', *Second Nature* (London, 1984), p. 100.

2 Peter Stallybrass and Allon White, *The Poetics and Politics of Transgression* (Ithaca, NY, 1986), pp. 49, 52.

3 Fraser Harrison, *Strange Land: The Countryside, Myth and Reality* (London, 1982), p. 60.

4 Cited in Erica Fudge, *Brutal Reasoning: Animals, Rationality, and Humanity in Early Modern England* (Ithaca, NY, 2006), p. 63; Stallybrass and White, *The Poetics and Politics of Transgression*, p. 51.

5 Francis Donald Klingender, *Animals in Art and Thought to the End of the Middle Ages* (Cambridge, MA, 1971), pp. 372–3; Stallybrass and White, *The Poetics and Politics of Transgression*, pp. 132–3, 147; Hy V. Luong, *Postwar Vietnam: Dynamics of a Transforming Society* (Lanham, MD, 2003), p. 119.

6 Milo Kearney, *The Role of Swine Symbolism in Medieval Culture* (Lewiston, NY, 1991), p. 322.

7 Kate Soper, *What is Nature?* (Oxford, 1995), p. 88; Alice Dawson, 'The Problem of Pigs', in *Geography and Ethics: Journeys in a Moral Terrain*, ed. J. D. Proctor and D. M. Smith (London and New York, 1999), pp. 193–205.

8 Stallybrass and White, *The Poetics and Politics of Transgression*, p. 50.

9 William Hedgepeth, *The Hog Book* (New York, 1978), pp. 82–102.

10 Carol J. Adams, *The Pornography of Meat* (New York, 2003), p. 161. The Trojan 'Evolve' campaign is online at trojanevolve.com (accessed 17 December 2008).

11 Thomas Hagey, *The Best of Playboar* (Buffalo, NY, 1996); Adams, *The Pornography of Meat*, pp. 104, 110.

12 Eric Partridge, *A Dictionary of Slang and Unconventional English: Colloquialisms and Catch-Phrases, Solecisms and Catachreses, Nicknames and Vulgarisms* [1937] (New York, 1984), p. 626.

13 Virginia DeJean Anderson, *Creatures of Empire: How Domestic Animals Transformed Early America* (Oxford, 2004); Scott Kaufman, *The Pig War: The United States, Britain, and the Balance of Power in the Pacific Northwest, 1846–72* (Lanham, MD, 2004).

14 James Buchan, 'My Hogs', *London Review of Books*, XXIII/20 (18 October 2001), p. 30–31; Hedgepeth, *The Hog Book*, p. 54.

15 Jennie M. Smith, *When the Hands Are Many: Community Organization and Social Change in Rural Haiti* (Ithaca and London, 2001), pp. 28–30.

16 Carl Fisher, 'Politics and Porcine Representation: Multitudinous Swine in the British Eighteenth Century', *Lit: Literature Interpretation Theory*, X/4 (March 2000), pp. 303–26.

17 *Oxford English Dictionary*, 'Pork Barrel', retrieved 22 October 2008.

18 Ben Zimmer, 'Who First Put "Lipstick on a Pig?"' *Slate.com*, online at www.slate.com/id/2199805 (accessed 12 September 2008).

19 National Public Radio programme, 6 March 2007; Dru Gladney, *Muslim Chinese: Ethnic Nationalism in the People's Republic* (Cambridge, MA, 1991).

20 Chris Brooke, 'Church School Renames Three Little Pigs to Avoid Offending Muslims', *Daily Mail*, 15 March 2007, online at www. dailymail.co.uk/news/article-442555/Church-school-renames-Three-Little-Pigs-avoid-offending-Muslims.html (accessed 10 March 2010).

21 'Pig Tactics Threatened', *Aftenposten*, 28 February 2007, online at www.aftenposten.no/english/local/article1665371.ece (accessed 30 September 2009).

22 Elliott Horowitz, 'Impurity and Danger', *The New Republic* (8 June 1998), pp. 40–44.

1 *Oxford English Dictionary*.

2 Marilyn Nissenson and Susan Jonas, *The Ubiquitous Pig* (New York, 1992), pp. 46–7.

3 Harold Wentworth and Stuart Berg Flexner, *Dictionary of American Slang* (New York, 1975).

4 Ibid.

5 Nissenson and Jonas, *The Ubiquitous Pig*, pp. 44–5. For a history of the Peppermint Pig, see www.saratogasweets.com.

6 Tom Dalzell, ed., *The Routledge Dictionary of Modern American Slang and Unconventional English* (New York, 2008), p. 503; Charles Earle Funk, *A Hog on Ice, and Other Curious Expressions* (New York, 1948).

7 Richard Hopwood Thornton, *An American Glossary: Being an Attempt to Illustrate Certain Americanisms upon Historical Principles* (Philadelphia, PA, 1912), vol. II, p. 750.

8 Eric Partridge, *A Dictionary of Slang and Unconventional English: Colloquialisms and Catch-Phrases, Solecisms and Catachreses, Nicknames and Vulgarisms*, 8th edn (New York, 1984).

9 *The Little Pig's Ramble from Home* [c. 1850]; Thomas Hood, *The Headlong Career and Woful* [sic] *Ending of Precocious Piggy* (London, 1859).

10 Beatrix Potter, *The Tale of Little Pig Robinson* [1930] (London, 2002) and *The Tale of Pigling Bland* [1913] (London, 2002); Ruth K. McDonald, *Beatrix Potter* (Boston, MA, 1986).

11 A. A. Milne, *Winnie the Pooh* [1926] (New York, 1991).

12 Bob Minzesheimer, 'Oink if you Love "Olivia"', *USA Today*, 13 February 2007, online at www.usatoday.com/life/books/news/2003–10-06-olivia_x.htm (accessed 30 September 2009).

13 E. B. White, 'Death of a Pig', *The Atlantic Monthly* (January 1948), pp. 28–33.

14 E. B. White, *Charlotte's Web* [1952] (New York, 1980).

15 Erica Fudge, *Animal* (London, 2002), p. 73.

16 Walter R. Brooks, *The Freddy Anniversary Collection* (Woodstock and New York, 2002); Adam Hochschild, 'That Paragon of

Porkers: Remembering Freddy the Pig', *New York Times Book Review*, 22 May 1994.

17 Dick King-Smith, *Chewing the Cud* (New York, 2001), pp. 6–7.

18 Dick King-Smith, *Babe: The Gallant Pig* (New York, 1995), originally published as *The Sheep Pig* (London, 1983).

19 Susan McHugh, 'Bringing Up Babe', *Camera Obscura*, XVII/1 (2002), pp. 153, 171. See also Susan McHugh, 'Clever Pigs, Failing Piggeries', *Antennae*, 12 (Spring 2010), pp. 19–24.

20 George Orwell, *Animal Farm* [1945] (New York, 1993), p. 18.

21 Morris Dickstein, 'Animal Farm: History as Fable', in *The Cambridge Companion to George Orwell* (Cambridge and New York, 2007), pp. 133–45; Orwell, *Animal Farm*, p. 114.

22 Cited in Michael Sheldon, *Orwell: The Authorized Biography* (New York, 1991), p. 371.

23 Dickstein, 'Animal Farm: History as Fable', pp. 133–45.

24 Orwell, *Animal Farm*, p. 90.

25 Sylvia Plath, *The Colossus and Other Poems* (New York, 1968); Ted Hughes, *New Selected Poems* (New York, 1982).

26 Denise Levertov, *Pig Dreams: Scenes from the Life of Sylvia* (Woodstock, VT, 1981), p. 38; Anne Dewey, '"The Art of the Octopus": The Maturation of Denise Levertov's Political Vision', *Renascence* (Fall 1997).

27 Philip Levine, *Not This Pig: Poems* (Middletown, CT, 1968).

28 David Tatham, *The Lure of the Striped Pig: The Illustration of Popular Music in America, 1820–1870* (Barre, MA, 1973), p. 146.

29 P. G. Wodehouse, 'Pig-Hoo-o-o-o-ey', in *The Most of P. G. Wodehouse* (New York, 1960), pp. 335–52.

30 Austin Scaggs, 'A Pig's Tale: Roger Waters Traces the History of Rock's Most Famous Prop', *Rolling Stone*, 29 May 2008, online at www.rollingstone.com/news/story/20877304/a_pigs_tale_roger _waters_traces_the_history_of_rocks_most_famous_prop (accessed 3 March 2010).

31 Leonard Maltin, *Of Mice and Magic: A History of American Animated Cartoons* (New York, 1980); Steve Schneider, *That's All Folks! The Art of Warner Bros. Animation* (New York, 1990).

32 *Three Little Pigs* [1933], Disney Archives, online at disney.go. com/vault/archives/movies/pigs/pigs.html (accessed 30 September 2009).

33 Susan King, 'Don't Hate the Swine: Great Movie Pigs', undated *Los Angeles Times* photo gallery, online at www.latimes.com/ business/careers/work/la-et-pigsmar05-pg,0,1752569.photo-gallery (accessed 30 September 2009).

34 See Frederick Cameron Sillar and Ruth Mary Meyler, *The Symbolic Pig: An Anthology of Pigs in Literature and Art* (Edinburgh and London, 1961); Musée provincial Félicien Rops Namur, online at www.museerops.be/tech/drawing/pornokrates.html (accessed 25 March 2010).

35 Sillar and Meyler, *The Symbolic Pig*, pp. 132–7.

36 Madeline McKenzie, 'Pigs on Parade to Kick Off Market Centennial Celebration', *The Seattle Times*, 31 May 2007, online at seattletimes.nwsource.com/html/pikeplacemarket/ 2003727482_nwwfestivalfocus31.html (accessed 30 September 2009); Karen Sandstrom, 'Going Whole Hog for Public Art: Painted Pigs Invade Cleveland', *The Plain Dealer*, 13 June 2007, online at blog.cleveland.com/entertainment/2007/06/ go_whole_hog_for_public_art_pa.html (accessed 30 September 2009); www.kingbladudspigs.org (accessed 05 April 2010).

37 'Cows, Pigs, Bats Spur Public-art Debate', *Deseret News*, 24 August 2003; Andrew Leicester, 'Cincinnati Gateway – Process', online at http://andrewleicester.com/case-study/ (accessed February 22, 2009); Erika Doss, *Spirit Poles and Flying Pigs: Public Art and Cultural Democracy in American Communities* (Washington, DC, 1995), p. 228.

38 Damien Hirst, *This Little Piggy Went to Market, This Little Piggy Stayed at Home*, 1996, steel, GRP composites, glass, pig and formaldehyde solution, electric motor, two glass tanks; 'Paul McCarthy at Hauser and Wirth', *Contemporary Art Daily*, 17 July 2009, online at www.contemporaryartdaily.com/ 2009/07/paul-mccarthy-at-hauser-wirth (accessed 30 September 2009).

39 See Daniel Birnbaum, 'Mice and Man: The Art of Carsten Höller and Rosemarie Trockel', *Artforum*, February 2001, pp. 114–19. The artists' website is online at n244.null2.net/502/geteiltes_haus/ (accessed 30 September 2009). Kira O'Reilly's *Inthewrongplaceness* is described in *Antennae: The Journal of Nature in Visual Culture*, 12 (Spring 2010), online at www.antennae.org.uk.

8 THE RETURN OF THE REPRESSED: WILD-LIVING PIGS

1 Global Invasive Species Database, 'Sus scrofa', online at www.issg. org/database/species/ecology.asp?si=73andfr=1andsts=sss (accessed 30 September 2009). See also John J. Mayer and I. Lehr Brisbin, Jr, *Wild Pigs in the United States* (Athens, GA, 2008).

2 United States Department of Agriculture, 'Wild Pigs: Hidden Danger for Farmers and Hunters', online at www.aphis.usda.gov/ lpa/pubs/pub_ahwildpigs.html (accessed 30 September 2009).

3 California Department of Fish and Game, 'Wild Pig Management Program', online at www.dfg.ca.gov/wildlife/hunting/pig/ (accessed 30 September 2009); *Guide to Hunting Wild Pigs in California*, online at www.dfg.ca.gov/publications/docs/ pigguide.pdf.

4 Craig Boddington, 'Hog Wild', *Petersen's Hunting*, April 2003.

5 'Wild Pig Hunt Aims to Save California Island Foxes', *National Geographic News*, online at news.nationalgeographic.com/news/ 2005/03/0316_050316_tvferalpigs_2.html (accessed 30 September 2009); Gregory W. Griggs, 'Eradication of Santa Cruz Island pigs deemed a success', *Los Angeles Times*, 30 August 2007; 'Feral Pigs Create Ecological Havoc on California's Channel Islands', *University of California Newsroom*, online at www.universityofcalifornia.edu/ news/article/3817 (accessed 30 September 2009); Gary W. Roemer, G. W., C. Josh Donlan and Franck Courchamp, 'Golden Eagles, Feral Pigs and Insular Carnivores: How Exotic Species Turn Native Predators Into Prey', *Proceedings of the National Academy of Sciences*, XCIX/2 (22 January 2002), pp. 791–6; Shannon Davis, 'Return of the Natives', *Backpacker* (June 2008), pp. 21–8.

6   'Hired Killer Stalks the Wild Pigs Plaguing Nebraska', *Wall Street Journal*, 30 May 2007.

7   Denise Grady, 'When Bad Things Come From "Good Food"', *New York Times*, 2 January 2007, online at www.nytimes.com/2007/01/02/health/nutrition/02seco.html?_r=1and8dpcandoref=slogin (accessed 30 September 2009); 'Pigs Source of Spinach E coli Outbreak, Say Investigators', *Medical News Today*, 28 October 28 2006, online at www.medicalnewstoday.com/articles/55300.php (accessed 30 September 2009).

8   The official website for Uncle Earl's is hosted by *Bayed Solid* magazine, online at www.bayedsolid.com (accessed 28 September 2009).

9   Danielle Ring, 'Hog-Dog Fights: Blood "Sport" Packaged as Family Entertainment', HSUS, at www.humanesociety.org/issues/hogdog_fighting/facts/hog-dog_bloodsport.html (accessed 3 March 2010).

10 *Fayette* [County, Georgia] *Citizen*, undated clipping in author's possession; A remarkably thorough account of the controversy over the canned hunt of the 'Monster Pig' is online at en.wikipedia.org/wiki/Monster_Pig (accessed 30 September 2009).

11 'The Mystery of Hogzilla Solved', *ABC News*, 21 March 2005, online at en.wikipedia.org/wiki/Monster_Pig (accessed 30 September 2009); 'Legendary 'Hogzilla' to Hit Big Screen', *The Washington Post*, 28 April 2007, online at www.washingtonpost.com/wp-dyn/content/article/2007/04/28/AR2007042800468.html (accessed 30 September 2009).

12 Department for Environment, Food and Rural Affairs, *Feral Wild Boar in England: An Action Plan* (London, 2008), online at www.defra.gov.uk. The British Wild Boar Organization can be found at www.britishwildboar.org.uk.

13 Phil Mercer, 'Australia Plagued by Feral Pigs', *BBC News*, 13 October 2007, online at news.bbc.co.uk/2/hi/asia-pacific/7042879.stm (accessed 17 March 2010); David Choquenot, John McIlroy and Terry Korn, *Managing Vertebrate Pests: Feral Pigs* (Canberra, 1996).

14 William Hedgepeth, *The Hog Book* (New York, 1978), p. 173.

Select Bibliography

Adams, Carol J., *The Pornography of Meat* (New York, 2003)

Albarella, Umberto, Keith Dobney, Anton Ervynck and Peter Rowley-Conwy, eds, *Pigs and Humans: 10,000 Years of Interaction* (Oxford, 2007)

Aloi, Giovanni, ed., *Antennae* 'Pig Issue', XII (Spring 2010), online at www.antennae.org.uk

Anderson, Arthur L., *Swine Management* (Chicago, 1950)

Anderson, Virginia DeJean, *Creatures of Empire: How Domestic Animals Transformed Early America* (Oxford, 2004)

Armstrong, Dan, and Dustin Black, *The Book of Spam: A Most Glorious and Definitive Compendium of the World's Favorite Canned Meat* (New York, 2007)

Ash, Russell, *The Pig Book* (New York, 1986)

Bass, S. Jonathan, '"How 'Bout a Hand for the Hog": The Enduring Nature of the Swine as a Cultural Symbol in the South', *Southern Cultures*, I/3 (Spring 1995), pp. 301–20

Belanger, Jerome D., *Raising the Homestead Hog* (Emmaus, PA, 1977)

Berger, John, 'Why Look at Animals', *About Looking* (New York, 1980), pp. 3–28

—, 'Animal World', *Second Nature* (London, 1984)

Biggle, Jacob, *Biggle Swine Book* (Philadelphia, PA, 1913)

Bingley, William, *Memoirs of British Quadrupeds* (London, 1809)

Bonera, Franco, *Pigs: Art, Legend, History* (Boston, MA, 1991)

Bowman, Sarah, and Lucinda Vardey, *Pigs: A Troughful of Treasures* (New York, 1981)

Brien, Donna Lee, and Adele Wessell, eds, *Media/Culture* 'Pig Issue', XIII/5 (October 2010), online at http://journal.media-culture. org.au/index.php/mcjournal/issue/view/pig

Brooks, Walter R., *The Freddy Anniversary Collection* (Woodstock and New York, 2002)

Buchan, James, 'My Hogs', *London Review of Books*, XXIII/20 (18 October 2001), pp. 30–31

Carlyon, David, *Dan Rice: The Most Famous Man You've Never Heard Of* (New York, 2004)

Cecelski, David, and Mary Lee Kerr, 'Hog Wild: How Corporate Hog Operations Are Slaughtering Family Farms and Poisoning the Rural South', *Southern Exposure*, XXII/3 (Fall 1992), pp. 8–15

Coe, Sue, *Dead Meat* (New York and London, 1996)

Crews, Harry, *A Childhood: The Biography of a Place* (New York, 1978)

Cronon, William, *Changes in the Land: Indians, Colonists, and the Ecology of New England* (New York, 1983)

—, *Nature's Metropolis: Chicago and the Great West* (New York, 1992)

Crosby, Alfred W., *The Columbian Exchange: Biological and Cultural Consequences of 1492* (Westport, CT, 1972)

—, *Ecological Imperialism: The Biological Expansion of Europe, 900–1900* (Cambridge and New York, 1986)

Dawson, Alice, 'The Problem of Pigs', in *Geography and Ethics: Journeys in a Moral Terrain*, ed. J. D. Proctor and D. M. Smith (London and New York, 1999), pp. 193–205

De Voe, Thomas Farrington, *The Market Assistant: Containing a Brief Description of Every Article of Human Food Sold in the Public Markets of the Cities of New York, Boston, Philadelphia, and Brooklyn* (New York, 1867)

D'Eramo, Marco, *The Pig and the Skyscraper: Chicago: A History of Our Future*, trans. Graeme Thomson, foreword by Mike Davis (London, 2002)

Dickens, Charles, *American Notes for General Circulation* (New York, 1868)

Dickstein, Morris, 'Animal Farm: History as Fable', in *The Cambridge Companion to George Orwell* (Cambridge and New York, 2007), pp. 133–45

Doss, Erika, *Spirit Poles and Flying Pigs: Public Art and Cultural Democracy in American Communities* (Washington, DC, 1995)

Duffy, John, *The History of Public Health in New York City, 1625–1866* (New York, 1968)

Dwyer, Peter D., and Monica Minnegal, 'Person, Place or Pig: Animal Attachments and Human Transactions in New Guinea', in *Animals in Person: Cultural Perspectives on Human-Animal Intimacies*, ed. J. Knight (Oxford and New York, 2005), pp. 37–60

Emery, Carla, *The Encyclopedia of Country Living: An Old Fashioned Recipe Book* (Seattle, WA, 2003)

Evans, E. P., *The Criminal Prosecution and Capital Punishment of Animals* (1906) (London and Boston, MA, 1988)

Fisher, Carl, 'Politics and Porcine Representation: Multitudinous Swine in the British Eighteenth Century', *Lit: Literature Interpretation Theory*, X/4 (March 2000), pp. 303–26

Fishwick, V. C., *Pigs: Their Breeding and Management* (London, 1944)

Foltz, Richard C., *Animals in Islamic Tradition and Muslim Cultures* (Oxford, 2006)

Freeman, Mike, 'Clarence Saunders: The Piggly Wiggly Man', *Tennessee Historical Quarterly* (Spring 1992), pp. 161–9

Fudge, Erica, *Animal* (London, 2002)

—, *Brutal Reasoning: Animals, Rationality, and Humanity in Early Modern England* (Ithaca, NY, 2006)

Garavini, Daniela, *Pigs and Pork: History, Folklore, Ancient Recipes* (Cologne, 1999)

Gladney, Dru, *Muslim Chinese: Ethnic Nationalism in the People's Republic* (Cambridge, MA, 1991)

Goodale, Jane C., *To Sing with Pigs is Human: The Concept of Person in Papua New Guinea* (Seattle and London, 1995)

Grettler, David, 'Environmental Change and Conflict over Hogs in Early Nineteenth-Century Delaware', *Journal of the Early Republic*, XIX/2 (1999), pp. 197–220

Hagey, Thomas, *The Best of Playboar* (Buffalo, NY, 1996)

Hall, Ian R., Gordon T. Brown and Alessandra Aambonelli, *Taming the Truffle: The History, Lore, and Science of the Ultimate Mushroom* (Portland, OR, 2007)

Harris, Joseph, *Harris on the Pig: Practical Hints for the Pig Farmer* [1883]

(New York, 1999)

Harris, Marvin, *The Sacred Cow and the Abominable Pig: Riddles of Food and Culture* (New York, 1987)

Harrison, Fraser, *Strange Land: The Countryside, Myth and Reality* (London, 1982)

Hartog, Hendrick, 'Pigs and Positivism', *Wisconsin Law Review* (July/August 1985), pp. 899–935

Hedgepeth, William, *The Hog Book* (New York, 1978)

Hollis, Gilbert R., and Stanley E. Curtis, 'General Characteristics of the US Swine Industry', in *Swine Nutrition*, ed. A. J. Lewis and L. L. Southern (Boca Raton, FL, 2001)

Hood, Thomas, *The Works of Thomas Hood, Comic and Serious, in Prose and Verse, with All the Original Illustrations*, ed. Tom Hood and Frances Freeling Hood Broderip (London, 1882)

—, *The Headlong Career and Woful [sic] Ending of Precocious Piggy* (London, 1859)

Hopmans, Susan, *The Great Murals of Farmer John Brand, Clougherty Meat Packing Co. in Vernon, California*, Photographs by Peter Kenner (New York, 1971)

Horowitz, Elliott, 'Impurity and Danger', *The New Republic* (8 June 1998), pp. 40–44

Horowitz, Roger, *Putting Meat on the American Table: Taste, Technology, Transformation* (Baltimore and London, 2005)

Horwitz, Richard P., *Hog Ties: Pigs, Manure, and Mortality in American Culture* (New York, 1998)

Huffman, Kirk, 'Pigs, Prestige and Copyright in the Western Pacific', *Explore*, XXIX/6 (February 2008), pp. 22–5

Hughes, Ted, *New Selected Poems* (New York, 1982)

Indiana Historical Bureau, 'Hoosier Hogs' (1994)

Jay, Ricky, *Learned Pigs and Fireproof Women* (New York, 1987)

Johnsen, Carolyn, *Raising a Stink: The Struggle over Factory Hog Farms in Nebraska* (Lincoln and London, 2003)

Johnson, Nathanael, 'Swine of the Times: The Making of the Modern Pig', *Harper's Magazine* (May 2006), pp. 47–56

Kalof, Linda, *Looking at Animals in Human History* (London, 2007)

Kaminsky, Peter, *Pig Perfect: Encounters with Remarkable Swine and Some Great Ways to Cook Them* (New York, 2005)

Karnasiewicz, Sarah, 'Going Whole Hog', Salon.com, 1 May 2007

Kaufman, Scott, *The Pig War: The United States, Britain, and the Balance of Power in the Pacific Northwest, 1846–72* (Lanham, MD, 2004)

Kearney, Milo, *The Role of Swine Symbolism in Medieval Culture* (Lewiston, NY, 1991)

King-Smith, Dick, *The Sheep Pig* (London, 1983)

—, *Chewing the Cud* (New York, 2001)

Klingender, Francis Donald, *Animals in Art and Thought to the End of the Middle Ages* (Cambridge, MA, 1971)

Larson, Greger, et al., 'Ancient DNA, Pig Domestication, and the Spread of the Neolithic into Europe', *Proceedings of the National Academy of Sciences*, 13 September 2007

LeDuff, Charlie, 'At a Slaughterhouse, Some Things Never Die', *New York Times*, 16 June 2000, reprinted in *Zoontologies: The Question of the Animal*, ed. Cary Wolfe (Minneapolis, MN, 2003), pp. 183–97

Lee, David, *The Porcine Canticles* (Port Townsend, WA, 1984)

Levertov, Denise, *Pig Dreams: Scenes from the Life of Sylvia* (Woodstock, VT, 1981)

Levine, Philip, *Not This Pig: Poems* (Middletown, CT, 1968)

Lobban, Jr, Richard A., 'Pigs and Their Prohibition', *International Journal of Middle East Studies*, XXVI/1 (1994), pp. 57–75

Lucas, Spencer G., and Robert J. Emry, 'Taxonomy and Biochronological Significance of *Paraentelodon*, a Giant Entelodont from the Late Oligocene of Eurasia', *Journal of Vertebrate Paleontology*, XIX/1 (March 1999), pp. 160–68

McHugh, Susan, 'Bringing Up Babe', *Camera Obscura*, XVII/1 (2002), pp. 149–87

—, 'Clever Pigs, Failing Piggeries', *Antennae*, XII (Spring 2010), pp. 19–24

Malcomson, Robert, and Stephanos Mastoris, *The English Pig: A History* (London, 1998)

Martinez, Steve W., 'Vertical Coordination in the Pork and Broiler Industries: Implications for Pork and Chicken Products', Economic Research Service, US Department of Agriculture, Report No. 777 (1999)

Matthews, Albert, 'Uncle Sam', *Proceedings of the American Antiquarian Society*, XXIX (Worcester, MA, 1909), pp. 21–55

Merback, Mitchell B., *The Thief, the Cross, and the Wheel: Pain and the Spectacle of Punishment in Medieval and Renaissance Europe* (London, 1998)

Midkiff, Ken, *The Meat You Eat: How Corporate Farming Has Endangered America's Food Supply* (New York, 2004)

Miles, William F. S., 'Pigs, Politics and Social Change in Vanuatu', *Society and Animals*, V/2 (1997), pp. 155–7

Milne, A. A., *Winnie the Pooh* (1926) (New York, 1991)

Mizelle, Brett, 'The Disappearance (and Slight Return) of Pigs in American Cities', *Antennae* 12 (Spring 2010), pp. 79-85

—, '"I Have Brought My Pig to a Fine Market": Animals, Their Exhibitors, and Market Culture in the Early Republic', in *Cultural Change and the Market Revolution in America, 1789–1860*, ed. Scott C. Martin (Lanham, MD, 2005), pp. 181–216

Moncrieff, Elspeth, with Stephen and Iona Joseph, *Farm Animal Portraits* (Woodbridge, Suffolk, 1997)

Montgomery, Sy, *The Good Good Pig: The Extraordinary Life of Christopher Hogwood* (New York, 2006)

Mooallem, Jon, 'Carnivores, Capitalists, and the Meat We Read', *The Believer* (October 2005)

Myers, Kathleen, *The Complete Guide for the Care and Training of Pet Potbellied Pigs* (New York, 2007)

Nelson, Sarah M., ed., *Ancestors for the Pigs: Pigs in Prehistory* (Philadelphia, 1998)

Niman, Nicolette Hahn, 'Pig Out', *New York Times*, 14 March 2007

Nissenson, Marilyn, and Susan Jonas, *The Ubiquitous Pig* (New York, 1992)

Oldridge, Darren, *Strange Histories: The Trial of the Pig, the Walking Dead, and Other Matters of Fact from the Medieval and Renaissance Worlds* (London and New York, 2005)

Olmsted, Frederick Law, *A Journey Through Texas; or, A Saddle-Trip on the Southwestern Frontier: with a Statistical Appendix* (New York, 1857)

Orwell, George, *Animal Farm* [1945] (New York, 1993)

Ownby, Ted, *Subduing Satan: Religion, Recreation, and Manhood in the*

Rural South, 1865–1920 (Chapel Hill, 1990)

Pinchbeck, William Frederick, *The Expositor; or, Many Mysteries Unravelled* (Boston, 1805)

Plath, Sylvia, *The Colossus and Other Poems* (New York, 1968)

Plutarch, *Moral Essays*, translated with an introduction by Rex Warner. Notes by D. A. Russell (Harmondsworth, England, 1971)

Pollan, Michael, *The Omnivore's Dilemma: A Natural History of Four Meals* (New York, 2006)

Porcher, Jocelyne, 'The Relationship between Workers and Animals in the Pork Industry: A Shared Suffering', *Journal of Agricultural Ethics*, 24 (2011), pp. 3–17

Porter, Valerie, *Pigs: A Handbook to the Breeds of the World*, illustrated by Jake Tebbit (Near Robertsbridge, East Sussex, 1993)

Potter, Beatrix, *The Tale of Little Pig Robinson* (1930) (London, 2002)

—, *The Tale of Pigling Bland* [1913] (London, 2002)

Pukite, John, *A Field Guide to Pigs* (New York, 1999)

Rath, Sara, *The Complete Pig: An Entertaining History of Pigs* (Stillwater, MN, 2000)

Salter, David, *Holy and Noble Beasts: Encounters with Animals in Medieval Literature* (Cambridge, 2001)

Sams, Ferrol, *Run with the Horsemen* (New York, 1982)

Sax, Boria, *Animals in the Third Reich: Pets, Scapegoats, and the Holocaust* (New York and London, 2000)

Schmalzer, Sigrid, 'Breeding a Better China: Pigs, Practices, and Place in a Chinese County, 1929–1937', *Geographical Review* 92.1 (January 2002), pp. 1-22

Schwenke, Karl, *In A Pig's Eye* (Chelsea, VT, 1985)

Secundus, Caius Plinius, *Pliny's Natural History: A Selection from Philemon Holland's Translation* (Oxford, 1964)

Shepard, S. M., *The Hog in America: Past and Present* (Indianapolis, 1886)

Sillar, Frederick Cameron, and Ruth Mary Meyler, *The Symbolic Pig: An Anthology of Pigs in Literature and Art* (Edinburgh and London, 1961)

Sinclair, Upton, *The Jungle* (1906) (New York, 1920)

Singer, Peter, and Jim Mason, *The Way We Eat: Why Our Food Choices Matter* (New York, 2006)

Smith, Jennie M., *When the Hands Are Many: Community Organization and Social Change in Rural Haiti* (Ithaca, NY, and London, 2001)

Smith, Robert E. F., and David Christian, *Bread and Salt: A Social and Economic History of Food and Drink in Russia* (Cambridge, 1984)

Soper, Kate, *What is Nature?* (Oxford, 1995)

Stallybrass, Peter, and Allon White, *The Poetics and Politics of Transgression* (Ithaca, NY, 1986)

Tatham, David, *The Lure of the Striped Pig: The Illustration of Popular Music in America, 1820–1870* (Barre, MA, 1973)

Tietz, Jeff, 'Boss Hog', *Rolling Stone*, 14 December 2006

Townsend, Jeannette, 'Pigs: A Demining Tool of the Future?', *Journal of Mine Action*, VII/3 (December 2003)

Toynbee, J.M.C., *Animals in Roman Life and Art* (London, 1973)

Trollope, Frances, *The Domestic Manners of the Americans* [1832] (New York, 1960)

Villas, James, *American Taste: A Celebration of Gastronomy Coast-to-Coast* (New York, 1982)

Walsh, Margaret, *The Rise of the Midwestern Meat Packing Industry* (Lexington, 1982)

—, 'From Pork Merchant to Meat Packer: The Midwestern Meat Industry in the Mid-Nineteenth Century', *Agricultural History*, LVI/1 (1982), pp. 127–37

Watson, Lyall, *The Whole Hog: Exploring the Extraordinary Potential of Pigs* (Washington, DC, 2004)

White, E. B., 'Death of a Pig', *The Atlantic Monthly* (January 1948), pp. 28–33

—, *Charlotte's Web* [1952] (New York, 1980)

Wigginton, Eliot, *The Foxfire Book* (New York, 1972)

Wilson, John S., 'Health Department', *Godey's Lady's Book*, 60 (February 1860)

Winfrey, Laurie Platt, *Pig Appeal* (New York, 1982)

Wiseman, Julian, *The Pig: A British History* (London, 2000)

Wodehouse, P. G., *The Most of P. G. Wodehouse* (New York, 1960)

Youatt, William, *The Hog; A Treatise on the Breeds, Management, Feeding, and Medical Treatment of Swine; with Directions for Salting Pork and Curing Bacon and Hams* (New York, 1855)

Associations and Websites

Grassroots International's Creole Pig Repopulation Program:
www.grassrootsonline.org/what-you-can-do/host-event/pig-party

The Humane Farming Association
www.hfa.org

Humane Society International
www.hsi.org/animals/pigs

Toronto Pig Save
http://torontopigsave.wordpress.com

People for the Ethical Treatment of Animals (PETA)
www.pets.org/issues/animals-used-for-food/pigs.aspx

PIG CULTURE

Porkopolis
Daniel E. Schultz's comprehensive site of pig knowledge and lore
throughout history
www.porkopolis.org

BBQ: A Southern Cultural Icon
xroads.virginia.edu/~class/MA95/dove/bbq.html

North American Potbellied Pig Association
www.petpigs.com

Draw a Pig Personality Test
http://drawapig.desktopcreatures.com

The Joy of Pigs
A PBS *Nature* documentary about pigs
www.pbs.org/wnet/nature/episodes/the-joy-of-pigs/
introduction/2123

Acknowledgements

A great many people have helped me research, write and illustrate this book. Friends both old and new contributed stories about, images of, and personal experiences of the human–pig relationship that have made this a far better and more interesting book than it would have been otherwise. As the late Alex Chilton put it: 'Thank you, friends. I wouldn't be here if it wasn't for you. I'm so grateful for all the things you helped me do.'

Special thanks to my students and colleagues in the Department of History and Program in American Studies at California State University Long Beach, who provided helpful references, contexts, illustrations, and support. I am indebted to the research support provided by CSULB in the form of assigned time, travel support, and a grant to help cover the costs of obtaining this book's many illustrations.

I am also grateful to the staff at the many libraries and museums that were of immense help, including the American Antiquarian Society, the Bancroft Library at the University of California Berkeley, the New York Public Library, the New York Historical Society and the Library Company of Philadelphia.

Eileen Luhr and Bernice Schrank read the entire manuscript and provided welcome advice and encouragement, as did Jonathan Burt, the editor of the Animal series. Michael Leaman, Harry Gilonis and Martha Jay at Reaktion Books were both patient and incredibly supportive in the long process of shepherding this book to completion.

Sarah Schrank has lived with this project for quite some time and his witnessed both my enthusiasm for pigs and the depressing reality of their circumscribed existence. I am grateful for her love and support, both at home and on the road. After all, events like the Ocmulgee Wild Hog Festival in south Georgia are not the most obvious of destinations for my Jewish, vegan wife.

Finally, I would like to dedicate this book to those around the world who are working to think and live differently with pigs and other non-human animals. More specifically, this book is for my mom, who has always encouraged critical thinking, respectful engagement and compassion for all creatures.

Photo Acknowledgements

The author and publishers wish to express their thanks to the below sources of illustrative material and / or permission to reproduce it.

Photo courtesy of the Accokeek Foundation, Accokeek, MD: p. 89; AFP / Getty Images: p. 96; photos American Antiquarian Society: pp. 52, 53, 55, 104, 134, 145, 147, 148, 159; collection of the author: pp. 71, 102, 107, 119, 141, 168; photos the author: pp. 9, 176; photo The Bancroft Library, University of California, Berkeley: p. 120; photo Bill Barber: p. 67; cover art Eddie Belchamber: p. 127 ["The contents of *oz* are not copyright. They may be reproduced in any manner, either in whole or in part, in any publication whatsoever (other than *The Sun* or *The News of the World*) without permission from the publishers. No rights reserved"]; Bibliothèque Nationale de France, Paris: p. 15 (foot); William Bingley, *Memoirs of British quadrupeds, illustrative principally of their habits of life, instincts, sagacity, and uses to mankind. Arranged according to the system of Linnæus* (London, 1809): p. 8 (top); Bodleian Library, University of Oxford: pp. 63 (MS. Laud Misc. 751), 118 (MS. Douce 346), 178 (MS. Rawl. liturg. e. 14); photo © Jacques Boyer / Roger-Viollet / Rex Features: p. 61 (top); The British Museum, London: pp. 28, 33 (top), 60 (Ms Royal 2 B VII), 87 (Ms Royal 2 B VII), 98 (British XVIIIC Unmounted Roy), 123 (Harley Ms. 4751); from the Comte de Buffon, *Histoire Naturelle . . .* (1799–1800): p. 17; from Joachim Camerarius, *Symbolorum ex re herbaria desumtorum centuria una collecta a Ioachimo Camerario medico Norimberg* (Nuremberg, 1590):

p. 117; Capitoline Museum, Rome: p. 30; Lewis Carroll, *Alice's Adventures in Wonderland* (London, 1865): p. 143; Castle Howard, Yorks: p. 165 (foot); © 1988 Sue Coe: p. 10; photo Cowan's Auctions Inc., Cincinnati, OH: p. 54; photo Philippe Desmazes / AFP / Getty Images: p. 88; photo Duke University Rare Book, Manuscript, and Special Collections Library, Durham, NC: p. 59; from *The Edinburgh Journal of Natural History, and of the Physical Sciences*, vol. I (1835–39): p. 14; John Engstead, MPTV Images: p. 161 (foot); photo F1 Online / Rex Features: p. 16; photo David Fenton: p. 128; photo courtesy Galerie St Etienne, New York: p. 10; photo GeorgHH: p. 139; photo Louis-Laurent Grandadam / Getty Images: p. 95; from *Grandpa Easy's The Little Pig's Ramble from Home* (Philadelphia, 1857): p. 145; photo used with permission from Grassroots International, www.GrassrootsOnline.org: p. 130; reproduced courtesy Thomas Hagley, Humorist, Waterloo, Ontario, Canada: p. 125; photo Hagley Museum & Library, Wilmington, DE: p. 67; Hebei Provincial Museum, Shijiazhuang, China: p. 18 (right); photo Jonathan Hordle / Rex Features: p. 72; photo Icon Images / Rex Features: p. 103; photo Imperial War Museum, London: p. 105; photo Isopix / Rex Features: p. 170; photo Menahem Kahana / Staff: p. 96; from Joseph Martin Kronheim, *My First Picture Book With Thirty-six Pages of Pictures Printed in Colours* (London, 1893): p. 144; photo Michael Leaman / Reaktion Books: p. 31; photo courtesy Jennifer Leistikow: p. 79; from *Leslie's Illustrated Newspaper*, 13 August 1859: p. 58; Library of Congress (Prints and Photographs Division): pp. 8 foot (Farm Security Administration – Office of War Information Photograph Collection), 46–49, 50–51, 56, 68, 101; from *The Life and Adventures of Toby, the sapient pig: with his opinions on men and manners. Written by himself* (London, *c.* 1817): p. 99; from James Long, *The Book of the Pig* (London, 1886): p. 21; from David Low, *The Breeds of the Domestic Animals of the British Islands Illustrated with Plates, From Drawings by Mr. W. Nicholson, Reduced from a Series of Portraits from Life, Executed for the Agricultural Museum of the University of Edinburgh, by Mr. W. Shiels*: vol. I: *The Horse, and the Ox* (London, 1842): pp. 19, 21, 23; photo Joshua Lutz: pp. 13, 106; rendering by Marc Marcuson,

University of Nebraska State Museum, Lincoln, NE: p. 15 (top); Collection of the Ministère des Affaires Sociales et de la Culture de la Communauté Française de Belgique: p. 166; photo courtesy collection of Patricia B. Mitchell (Food History.com): p. 62; Musée des Beaux-Arts de la Ville de Paris, Petit Palais: p. 129; Musée Carnavalet, Paris: p. 37, 132 (photos © Musée Carnavalet / Roger-Viollet / Rex Features); Museo della Civiltà Romana, Rome: p. 33 (foot); Museum of Fine Arts, Boston: p. 165 (top); from Eadweard Muybridge, *Animal Locomotion: an Electro-Photographic Investigation of Consecutive Phases of Animal Movements 1872–1885* (Philadelphia, 1887): p. 86; photo The New York Public Library (Rare Books Division – Astor, Lenox, and Tilden Foundations): p. 19; National Museum, Athens: p. 34; photo Collection of the New-York Historical Society: p. 58; photos © Jack Nisberg / Roger-Viollet / Rex Features: pp. 66, 76; photo David Noon: p. 180; photo F. A. Pazandak Photograph Collection, North Dakota Institute for Regional Studies, North Dakota State University, Fargo, ND: p. 74; photo © Petit Palais / Roger-Viollet / Rex Features: p. 129; The Pierpont Morgan Library, New York: pp. 24, 173; photo © Roger-Viollet / Rex Features: pp. 20, 33 (foot), 57, 61 (foot), 82, 90, 124, 155; photo Arthur Rothstein: p. 8 (foot); photos Jeffrey Ryan: pp. 119, 125, 141, 168; from *Some Very Gentle Touches to Some Very Gentle-Men, By a Humble Country Cousin of Peter Pindar, Esq.* (New York, *c.* 1820): p. 53; from *Speculum Humanae Salvationis* (Basel, 1496): p. 35; photo © Dennis Stock, Magnum Photos: p. 121; photo Keren Su / China Span: p. 27; photo courtesy Tasende Gallery, La Jolla, CA: p. 169; photo US National Library of Medicine, Bethesda, MD: p. 108; photo Charles Van Schaick / Wisconsin Historical Society: p. 45; from *The Wasp*, vol. V, Aug.–Dec. 1880: p. 120; photo Weed: p. 127; Yale University Art Gallery, New Haven, CT: p. 18 (left); photos Zoological Society of London: pp. 14, 21, 23.

Index